I'M NOT NO ONE

PROLOGUE

This book was created to give our Ambassadors a venue through which their voices could be heard. Our children spoke. Some screamed. Now it is our turn to listen.

PROLOGUE

Youth Ambassadors, established in 2010, is an innovative collaboration of community partners in the Kansas City metropolitan area who joined forces to implement a State-of-the-art educational program for underserved teenagers.

Youth from both sides of the state line, Kansas and Missouri, are hired as Ambassadors of their neighborhoods during non-school hours, when teenagers are most vulnerable to negative influences. With direction from community leaders, our youth build on their knowledge of what is happening on the streets and learn how they can stand up for positive change.

The Youth Ambassadors program believes that youth need to take ownership of their communities — the good, the bad, the ugly and the beautiful — before effective change can occur. To this end, our Ambassadors explore their communities through digital photography, documentary production, writing, art, historical references and intimate interviews. In the process, they explore themselves, their roles in the community and the issues about which they feel most passionate.

Meaningful connections and relationships between youth and positive role models are encouraged, and lines of communication and a venue through which students both give and receive respect and genuine concern are established when personal writings are shared, and visual representation of personal thought and feeling is explored through therapeutic art.

In addition, Ambassadors are taught life skills, including financial responsibility, anger management, conflict resolution, recognition of impediments to success, smart choices, leadership skills and business etiquette. Youth Ambassadors are our future community leaders. We work to empower them.

PROLOGUE

Broken Little Bird

Words of Hope and
Despair from the
Youth of Kansas City

KAREN BALL
former Associated Press reporter

DAVID VON DREHLE
editor-at-large for Time magazine

PROLOGUE

Perhaps the desolate and scary neighborhoods of America's inner core are remote and abstract to you. Or perhaps you've driven through, stepping on the gas pedal just a little harder to make a quick escape, and looking straight ahead as boarded-up houses, vacant lots, shabby or barren storefronts passed namelessly by.

There is no ignoring — no speeding past — the remarkable collection of unedited writings in *I'm Not No One*. This book contains reflections, essays and poems written by young people in some of those troubling places. They are voices from the world we prefer to ignore. Often eloquent, always riveting, they are the "Youth Ambassadors" whose words are finally heard thanks to a five-year-old program for at-risk teens in the greater Kansas City area.

Youth Ambassadors is an innovative jobs program for kids of high school age — not make-work jobs, but make-whole jobs. Promising young people, at risk of failure, are paid to take command of their own lives, to claim ownership in their communities, to attend classes and shape them by their participation, to say what is really happening on their streets and to make positive change.

This program started in 2010 in the hardscrabble, racially diverse neighborhood of Kansas City, Kan., known as Argentine. It is a place where family is respected, and yet so many young adults worry that they will never get a job — especially the young adults who are not legal immigrants. College is a distant figment. In the years since then, the Youth Ambassadors program has drawn their voices from the shadows, as the program expanded to the neighborhoods known as Central, Rosedale, Turner and across the state line to the Ivanhoe neighborhood in Kansas City, Mo., a similarly troubled, neglected area where young people see few ways out.

The Ambassadors initiative works to open their eyes. Through digital photography, writing, art, documentaries and interviews, young women and men explore their own lives and their roles in the community. Paid a stipend for their work, they learn about financial responsibility. They learn how to interview for a job — to shake hands, speak clearly and look a potential employer in the eye. For some it is the first time they have been given the genuine respect they deserve as future leaders of their communities. And the first time they have begun to understand the hard work that leadership entails.

Writing is especially hard for many of these young Ambassadors. English is often a second language. Telling the truth can be a perilous gamble. Yet here they are, fearless and bold, telling their stories. Cries of pain, yes, but also poetic and urgent declarations of hope. In their own words, these young adults share the raw reality of their lives, alongside dreams for their futures:

"I am from a broken family to a family that is now healed. I am from a place where I can dream big and never give up my hopes."

Writes a 16-year-old, angry and fearful for her abused and sick mother:

"No one knows, not my friends, not my cousins, no one. So I call myself a broken little bird, running, flying, trying to find answers just so I can find my way out to be free from all the pain. I would do anything, anything in the world, to see my mom happy again. But all I can do is pray to God and believe that everything will be okay...I'm going make my mom's dreams that she wants for me come true."

We see the shadow of violence:

"One of my best friends died in November because of a drive by. ... That's when I slowly started backing away. ... So my mom's been pulling me into church, and I'm kind of liking it."

We hear moments of hard-won pride:

"My parents, brother and I came across the border when I was older than five. Without an idea of the language, no house and no job they thought we would collapse, but look at us now. My dad has his own business and mom a beautiful home. The kids? Those poor doubted souls are top of the class and getting running awards."

We hear the thankfulness they feel for their single moms, and the overworked grandmas who have stepped in to help. The gratitude is overpowering; their anguish over missing fathers is gut-wrenching:

"I wish I could see him more but he's always out running the streets. He pretends like he's broke and never has money. How could you have a nice car with rims on it but you can never put money in your oldest child's pocket?"

Who among us knows the feeling as a child of having a gun to their head, of having to check on Mom to see if she's overdosed, the pressure of being "jumped in," or to accept the gang life?

Riveting and lyrical, these dispatches bring you up close and personal to the challenges facing our at-risk youth, and their determination to rise above both for themselves and their community.

PROLOGUE

The voices of the youth in this book cover such a broad range of topics and emotions. These heartfelt writings reflect life experiences from young people who have experienced so much — often too much — on the cusp of adulthood. Their words are both educational and insightful.

I applaud Youth Ambassadors for giving a voice to these young people. It makes such a difference for youth when they know they are heard, when they feel that people care what they think. The writings contained in this book are worth reading — you come away with a better understanding of what are often the harsh realities of their world and what they felt, while getting a real glimpse into their lives.

JIM COOK
President
Children International

PROLOGUE

As I read through the stories that fill the pages of this book, I am reminded just how many dreams are built in Kansas City but, unfortunately, vanish right before our eyes. They are the dreams of mothers and the dreams of fathers. Dreams of our young women and dreams of our young men. Dreams that once held promise and potential hang now in the balance and sadly, for too many, were never even imagined.

What is at stake for our children is everything, and I have no greater concern. I believe it is simply immoral to have citizens in this community, or any community, who cannot read in this day and age. Regardless of where you live, regardless of your occupation, having your own children or not, our future is tied to the abilities of our citizens and to the dreams that fill their souls. What our children become as they go forward is quite literally in our hands and should always weigh heavily on our hearts.

As you read through the stories in this book, do so with the understanding that our best strategy for decreasing crime and increasing the success of our young people is to increase the employment opportunities that exist for them. If you have heard me speak around our city, then you have probably heard me say that the best crime-fighting tactic is a job. Education is the cornerstone on which all dreams are built. Knowing what opportunities exist in the world, and having the tools to seize them, sets our minds, our hearts and our success in motion.

The youth of Kansas City depend on us. Too many of them have been let down. Where parents have forgotten them, where schools have failed them, where the opportunity for a brighter day and a better way was never even presented to them, this is where we must step in. Our unwavering commitment to education becomes our steadfast commitment to them. It determines what our young people will become, and it is for all of us, the most accurate prediction of what the future holds.

SYLVESTER "SLY" JAMES
Mayor of Kansas City, Mo.

I WANT TO BE

HEARD

There is one thing that I want out of this crazy life I live. There is only one thing that I want from this cold world. There is one thing in my way. YOU, you who told me that kids of my background do not have enough ambition or focus to make it in life. YOU, you who allow yourselves to be content with that ghetto living, because you've been told that there's nothing else out there for you. You who did not seek the knowledge necessary to find out what else is out there. You who claimed you were my friend and yet tossed me to the side when I told you that I was better than that drug selling, gang affiliated life. You who did not encourage me to do better, to tell me to keep pushing. You who disowned me after I said I could no longer live in this run down apartment with gun shots and police sirens keeping me up at night. It's you - you are my obstacle. And you may step aside, because my future awaits me. ■

I'm a 16-year-old boy who sees the world as a game, and I'm one of its players. I walk around sometimes mad at the world, so I keep my head down and my hood over my head. I hate attention when I really don't deserve it. I'm the type of young man who leaves his heart and feelings at home locked deep and hidden away. To be honest, I would really like to take my feelings and emotions, set them on fire, shoot them to death, and bury them. I have cool memories filled with outstanding goals, but those wipe away very quickly. I'm basically the type of boy who hates the morning and loves the darkness, one who sits high above the ground and stares at the dark sky filled with stars and the moon. I'd rather be alone then be around a group of kids. I cherish very little: my family, football, and music. Football is basically a way to get all my anger out, so I would describe it as a medicine. Now, don't get me wrong, Christ has always been in my life. My grandfather raised me in his own church, so me being Christian is 100%. ■

I was chillin' inside wit two of my friends. My brother was outside on the front porch. I think he was talkin' on the phone. All of a sudden I hear a gunshot, jus one, and it's not that unusual, but it sounded really close. I really thought nothin' of it at first until one of my friends looked out the front window to see my brother laying there wit a pretty decent size blood stain on his shirt. He had the phone with him, so the ambulance was called right after, but they were takin' their time. When they got there I remember lookin' my brother in the eyes, but I didn't know if he was fading away or trying not to panic. I was scared to ask, but as they took him to the hospital I started to have faith. And like a soulja he came out on top. ■

IT'S YOU – YOU ARE MY OBSTACLE. AND YOU MAY STEP ASIDE, BECAUSE MY FUTURE AWAITS ME.

The word nigga is a stupid one. It is an insult to blacks everywhere. The year is 2012 not 1776, a day of freedom, liberty and no slavery. So to people who say nigga – it is stupid. ■

My generation is out of control. They went from fighting their fights with fists to fighting their fights with straps. Pulling the trigger doesn't make you a man. If anything it makes you a boy. Grow up and open your eyes and realize a bullet has no eyes. You could hit anything and anyone. ■

PULLING THE TRIGGER DOESN'T MAKE YOU A MAN.

This summer I lost too many friends from things like overdoses to gunshot wounds, simply because they were at the wrong place at the wrong time or because of the saying YOLO. YOLO was meant to motivate people to follow their dreams not to be used as an excuse to do stupid and crazy things. Rest in peace to all those that died this summer. ■

Some think of me as stupid, but I'm not. They are the ones. I am who I am in my own right, and God will guide me in his light. So to you all – peace, cause I'm just me. ■

I am from a loving mother that has overcome addiction. I am from a broken family to a family that is now healing. I am from a place of strong convictions and helping out my community. I am from a place where I can dream big and never give up my hopes. I hope to become a writer and write children's books for the children that have nothing. ■

13

14

15

NO ONE EMPOWE... SO I EMP... MYSELF.

IAS
RED ME,
OWER

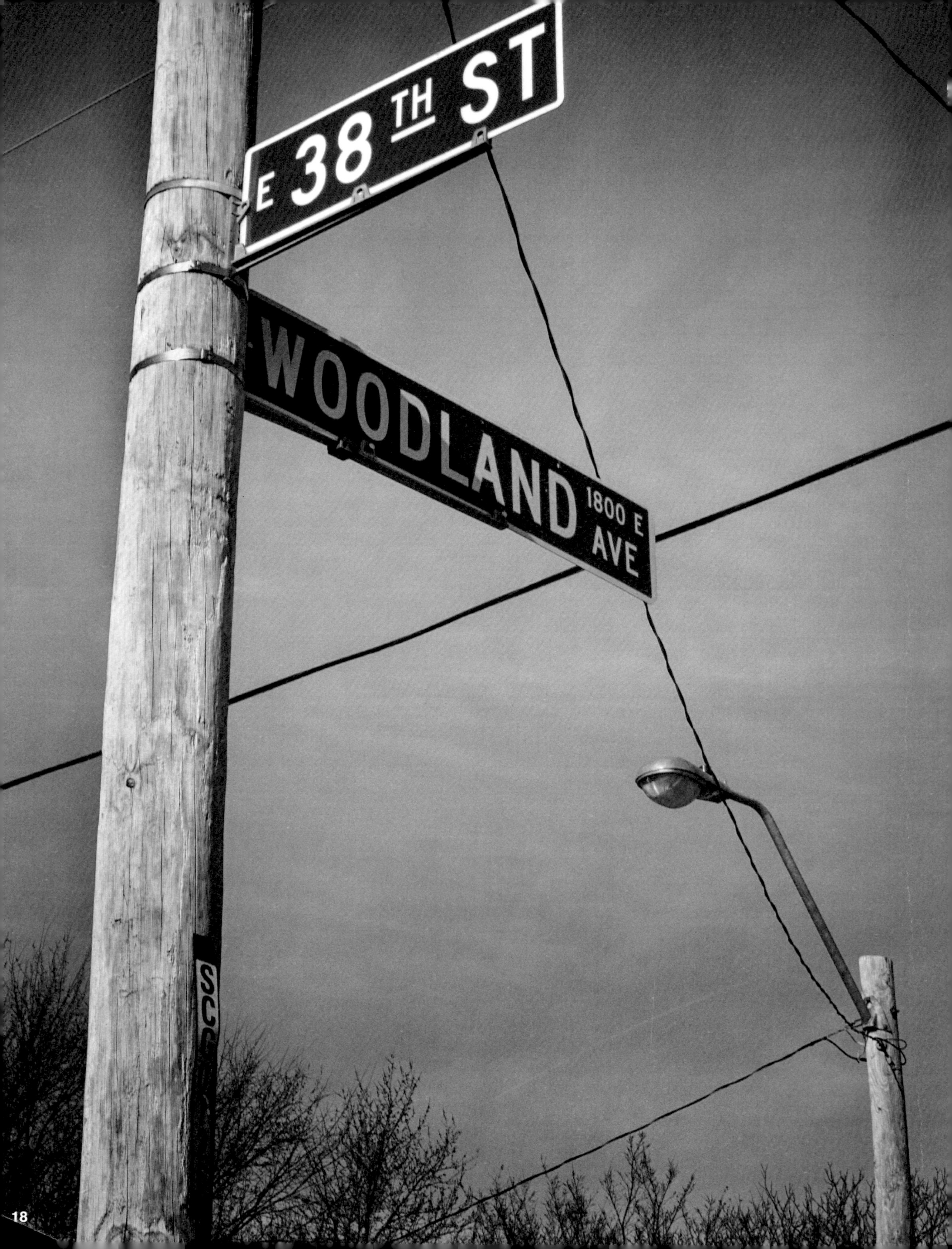
E 38 TH ST
WOODLAND 1800 E AVE

No one has empowered me, so I empower myself. It's been times when I've been told I'm not going to amount to nothing. But I looked past it all. I won't be nothing. I'm not going nowhere in life. I look at ways to improve myself and keep pushing until I reach my goals. When I was younger I used to wanna give up, but someone once told me that God won't give me something I can't handle, so I keep believing in myself, no letting negativity pull me down, learning from every mistake I make. ∎

I SHOT A SHOTGUN ON THE 4TH. I DON'T KNOW WHY I DID IT. I JUST DID. IT MADE MY EARS RING, MY WRIST HURT, AND I DAMN NEAR FELL. THIS MORNING I HEARD ABOUT AN 11-YEAR-OLD GIRL GETTING SHOT ON ACCIDENT. IT DIDN'T MAKE ME FEEL GUILTY, BUT I DID FEEL FOR HER.

I don't know if I'll be able to go to college, because I was not born here. Well, I could, to a private one. That's a lot of money though. So, I am working my hardest in academics and sports to get a scholarship, so I can give my parents, brothers, and sister a better life. Later on in life - my family. This puts a lot of stress on me sometimes, and I crack really badly under stress. The second thing is that I think I might have breast cancer. We're going to the doctors a lot to make sure I don't, but nothing is positive or negative. This makes it hard, because I look at my life and I'm like, "wow, what if I am sick? Am I really going to leave all of this soon?" What makes me sad, though, is that I wanted to make a BIG impact in the world, and I might not be able to. ∎

I love how god made me out to be, but there are some things that i would change, like the shape of my head. I get made fun of a lot because of it sometimes. I pay no mind to it, but sometimes it gets to me. I hate the fact that back when I was younger the only person that understood me was my cousin. I hate that God took my cousin away when I needed her the most. I hate that I have a girlfriend, and we have been dating for almost two years, and she still doesn't understand me. I hate that for 11 years I thought my godmother was my mother. I hate that I didn't know I had a brother until five years ago. I hate that I never had a father figure around to show me right from wrong. I hate that I'm so young, but I feel so old. I hate that I'm smaller then most people my age. I really hate that I cut all my hair off! I had lots of hair that I truly miss. I hate how people expect so much of me, and when I don't give them what they want, they get upset with me. I know I'm a smart kid, and I know I can do anything I want to, but I just don't like being pushed to do it. I hate that the only sport I am good at is football. I hate fighting. I mean, don't get me wrong, I can fight, I just really don't like to. I hate that my family is full of gang-bangers, and killers and drug-dealers. I hate that the gang life caught a hold of me and won't let go. I hate my school. I hate how people judge me because of the color of my skin. I hate that I get really shy around people I don't know. I hate that my mom raised me and my big brother as a single parent. I hate when people stare at me. I hate that my dad has so many kids but takes care of none of them. But what makes me happy the most is knowing that I have lots of people that love me for who I am. It makes me happy that I have friends that are here for me. ■

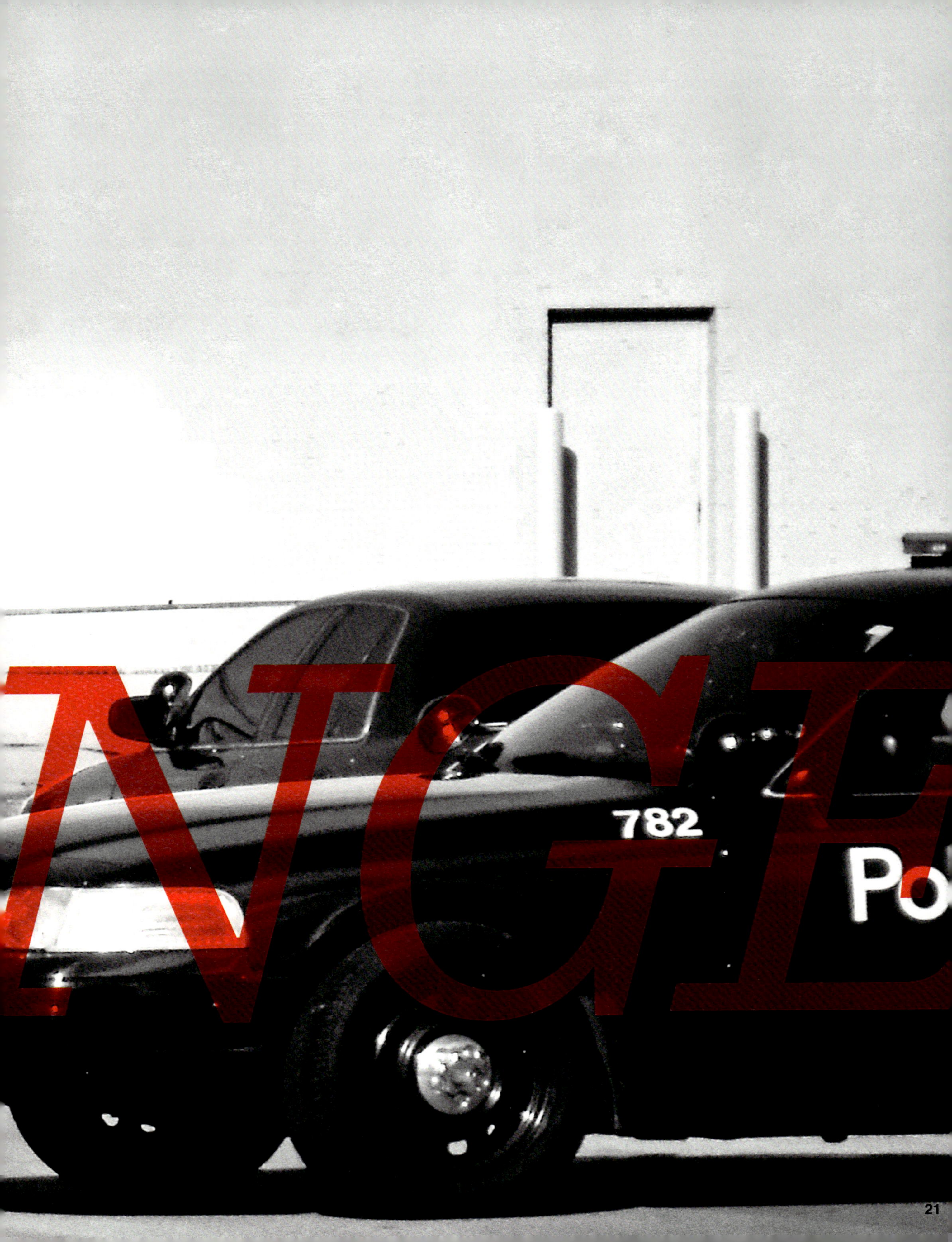
NGE
782
Po

As a kid I never liked school. Every day was getting worse. Every day I hated the teachers more and hated school more. I got older and started to skip. We would just hang out at my house or my cousin's house. The more I skipped, the more work I wouldn't do. I'd fall back, and I'd feel like I couldn't catch up. I felt like there was no reason to go anymore. So I just quit going as soon as the school year was over. I chose to drop out. When the next school year started, I just went up to the school and dropped out. I was fifteen.

As the year went by, I wasn't doing nothing. Ya, dropping out of school ain't cool. All your friends are in school and all the girls too. When you try to get a job, nobody wants to hire a dropout. They think you'll just quit. So you spend a lot of time doing your own thing. There's nothing to do; you just sleep or play video games, and you ain't got no money to do the things you want to do. For a lot of jobs you need at least a GED. Now I wish I never dropped out. I hope kids read this and they don't just think I'm bullshitting. School is one of the most important steps in life.

I'm seventeen now, trying to see what move I should do to get me in a better situation and get me on my feet. As I write this, I think in my head things would be different if I stayed in school; how I would not need a job cuz I'm in school, and maybe my people would act different with me. But no one from my family has made it to college. They dropped out. Ya, if I stayed in school, next year I could have been walking across that stage with that square hat, but I guess I'm never gonna feel that. ■

I began my life as a quiet little girl. I was sweet, innocent and naïve. I sat back and watched as my family began to self-destruct. My mother was a teen mom by the age of 16. I was her last born at the age of 22. My mother had 5 children over the course of 7 years by four different men. As I got older, I watched my mother marry a crack head who seemed to be a "good man." I never understood what her criteria was for a "good man." I watched my mother cry every night and lash out on my siblings to release frustration caused by her "good man" who was an addicted crack head who constantly stole Christmas presents and the birthday money. Then one day, I sat outside of my home while this "good man" beat my sister, because he didn't have money to buy more crack. At the age of seven I sat outside my home and listened to my sister scream for help. By the age of eight, I watched this "good man" walk back into my home and one by one force my siblings, the closest people to me, to leave not only my home but my family too. And now I'm stuck at home, alone everyday with this "good man." ■

Fuck it. I'm sick of being here. I can't take it. Jobs ain't hiring, and they trying to make it hard for me to support my baby. Lately I been working on doing things on my own, and I been kind of busy, so I ain't been picking up the phone. Heaven would be a better place then being here on earth. Home is a place I would like to call heaven, cause up there you ain't got to worry bout niggas gossiping and the other niggas jeffing. Blessings is what I call waking up every day with clothes on yo back, shoes on yo feet and food on yo plate. ■

My perfect world is a world where abortion doesn't exist. My perfect world is a world where a black man would take care of his responsibilities and wouldn't wish his kids were never born. My perfect world is a world where a 15-year-old girl is not being pimped out by her mama or step daddy just because they need money. My perfect world is a world where a black 16-year-old male does not have to remember the days he spent in a foster home abused, no food, and hand me downs. My perfect world is where AIDS doesn't exist or where disease is not spread through sexual contact. My perfect world is a world where you can walk around with a smile on your face and your head held high. My perfect world is where I can look at my mom and she would be proud of me. My perfect world is a world with peace and silence, a place that I can just go sit down and relax, where I can walk outside and not have the risk of being shot, because I'm wearing a certain color. Even though this perfect world will never exist, I wish it could. ■

WITHOUT FOOTBALL, I WOULD BE ANOTHER BLACK KID ON THE STREETS GANG BANGING OR SELLING DRUGS.

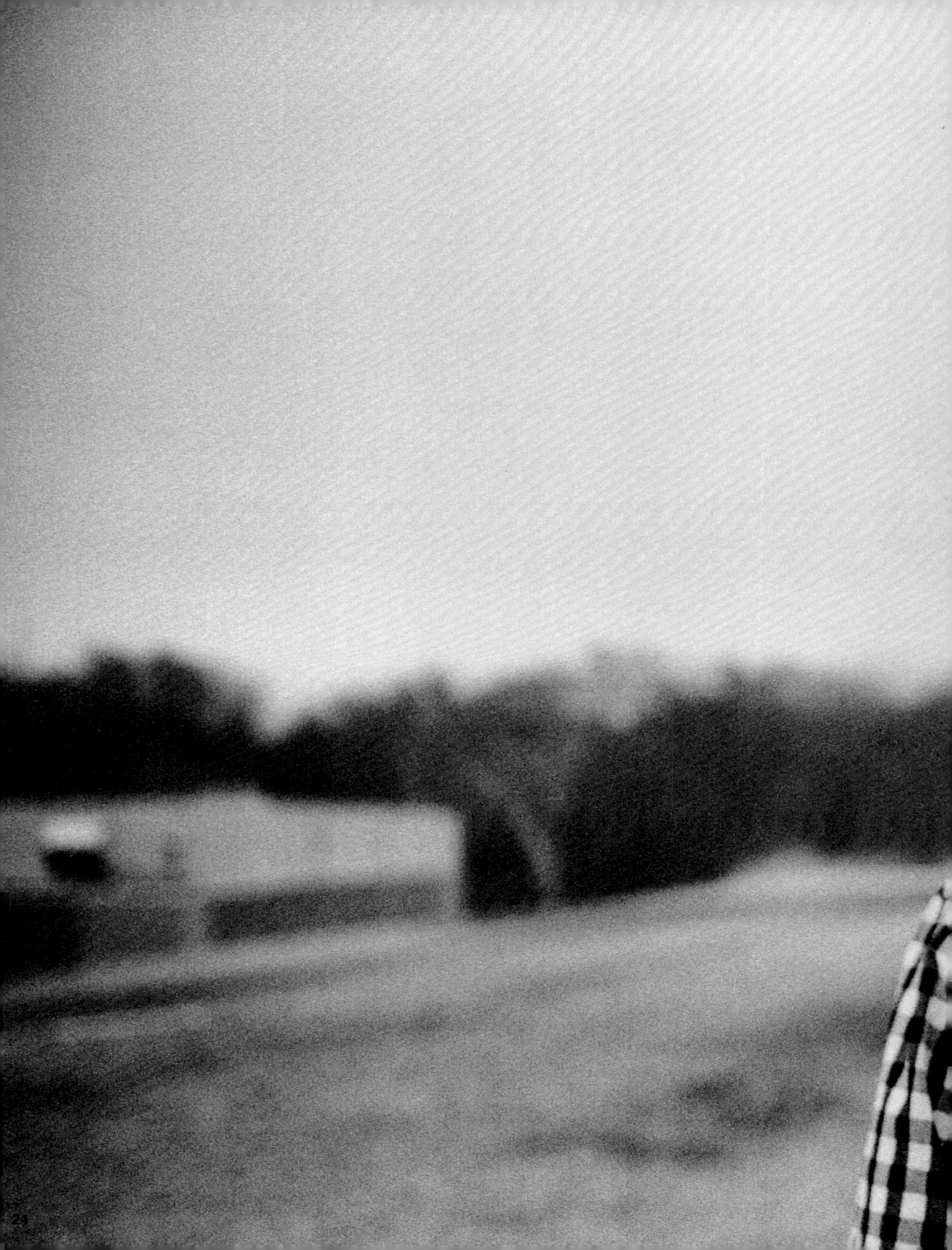

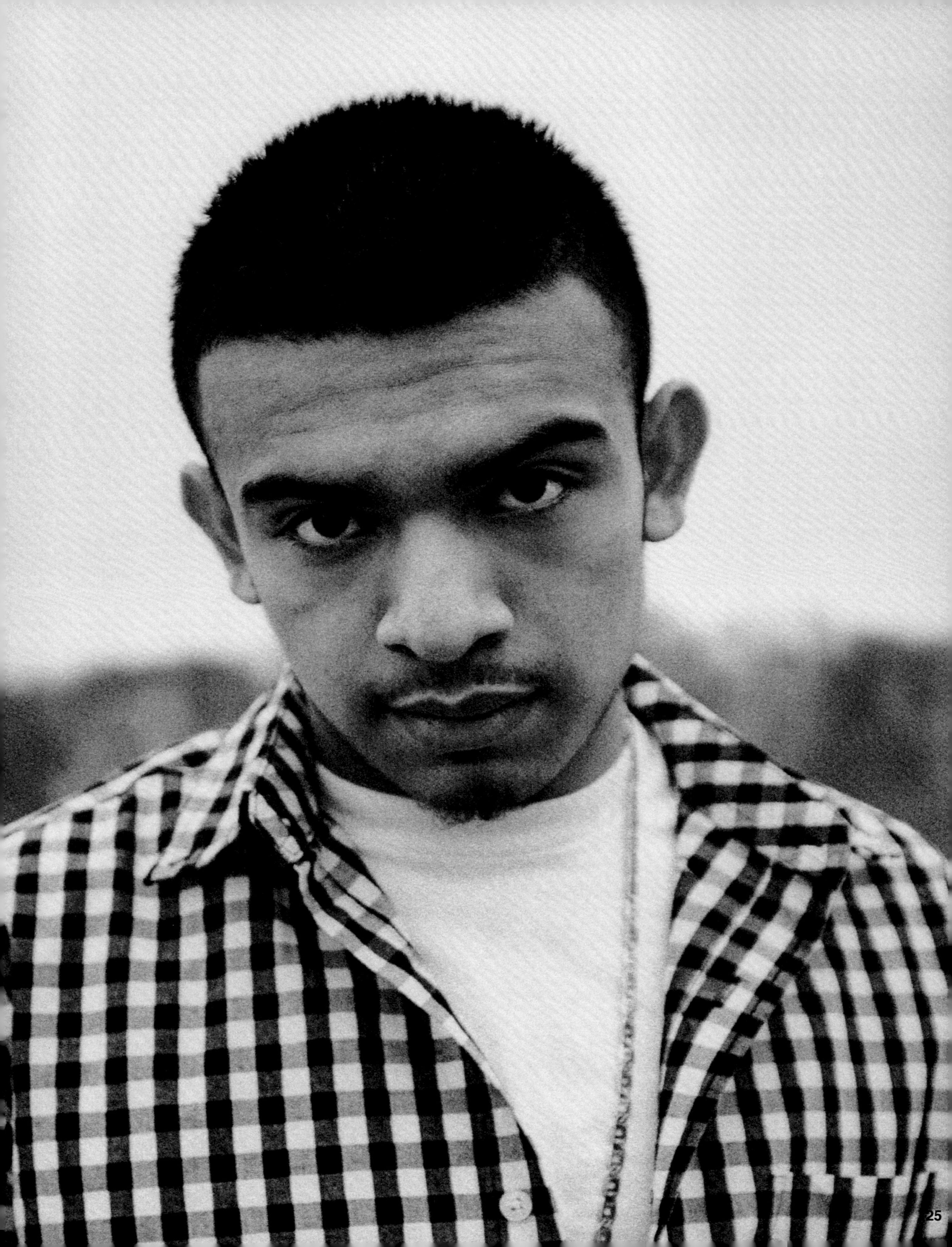

SURROUND YOURSELF WITH PEOPLE WHO…

MAKE IT. I WANNA MAKE IT. WHO WANT SEE YOU MAKE IT.

I was in the backyard playing with my brother. I was little again. We were climbing the trees to see who could climb the highest. We were both live, little monkeys. We loved to climb, hang or swing on the trees, until my mom would come outside and tell us to come inside to wash our hands for dinner. I was having a good dream of the way things used to be until the sound of my parents arguing and the smell of cigarettes brought me back to reality. I wake up to this every day, my parents arguing about money, bills and food. I wish it didn't have to be this way, living paycheck to paycheck, having to struggle to get the things we need to get us by. I know life isn't perfect, and I don't expect it to be, nor do I want it to be, but I know it can be better than how it is now, and I'm working hard to get it that way. That's one of my many goals in life. I know I have to work hard to get to where I want to be, and I know one day I'll get to were I'm going, and it will all be worth it. In the end it will all be worth it. ■

MY NEIGHBORHOOD IS MESSY AND DIRTY. DURING THE DAY IT'S FILLED WITH CRACK HEADS PLAYING CARDS, YELLING DOWN THE BLOCK. KIDS NEVER HAVE DREAMS; THEY ARE JUST LIVING BY THE DAY.

June 6th, 2011 my favorite beloved cousin was gunned down on 44th and Tracy. He was shot over 36 times and lived for 27 minutes. He tried to drive himself to a nearby hospital but failed in doing so. He died leaving, and departed earth, went into his earthly slumber, and walked with his head up high through the tall golden gates of heaven while being welcomed by the Lord himself, our Savior Jesus Christ. It's hard for my aunt to see her son die at the age of 26. In a perfect world a mother would never have to sit in the front row of a funeral service to see her child, dead and stiff, laying there lifeless in a casket. Rest in Peace Reggie Allen. I miss you cousin. ■

CRACK HEAD HOTEL

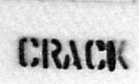

CRACK HEAD HOTEL

Fuck THE POLICE

FUCK 'SUCK' SMOKE DOPE

PAIN MAKES IT HARD TO TRUST.

PAIN MAKES ME FRAGILE.

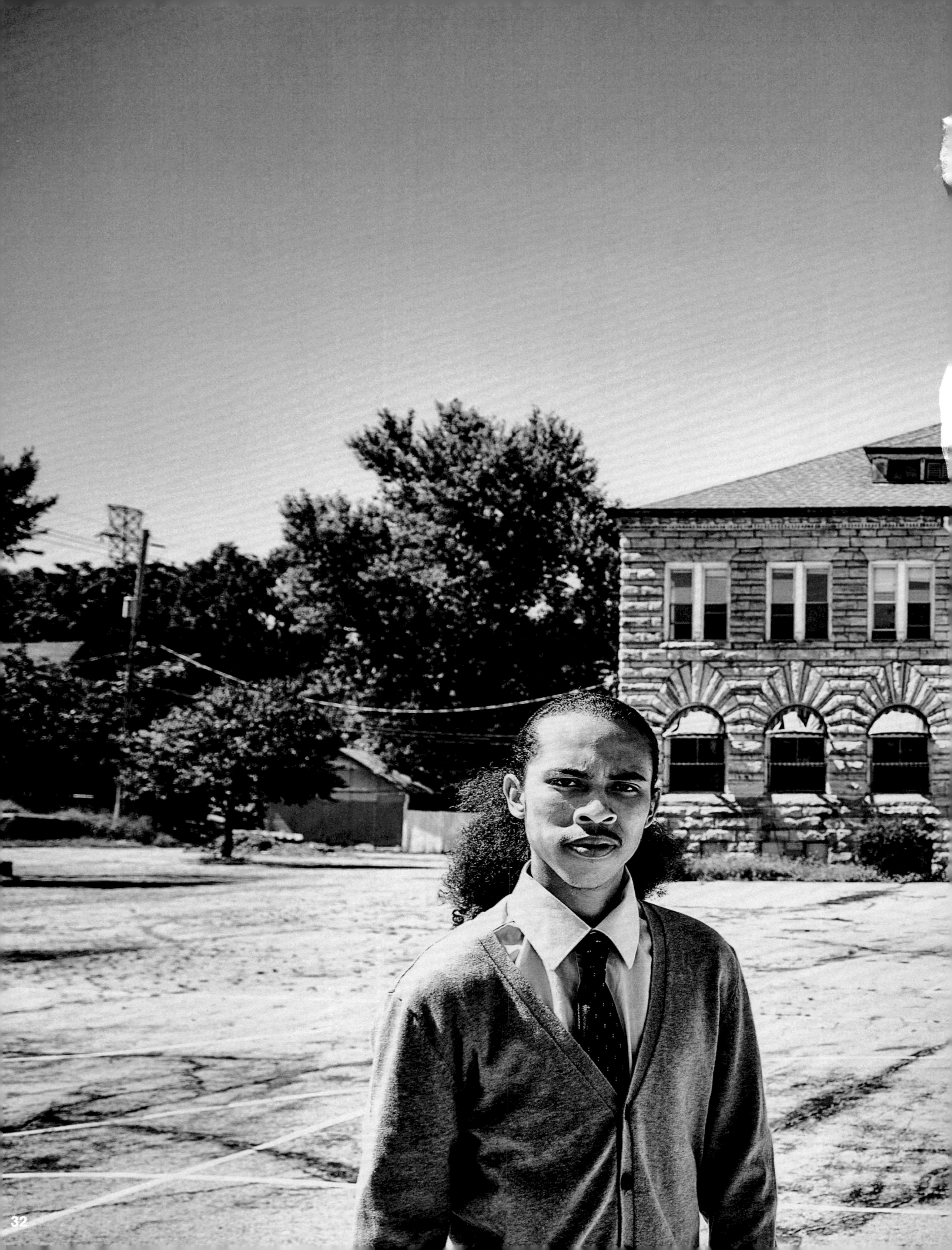

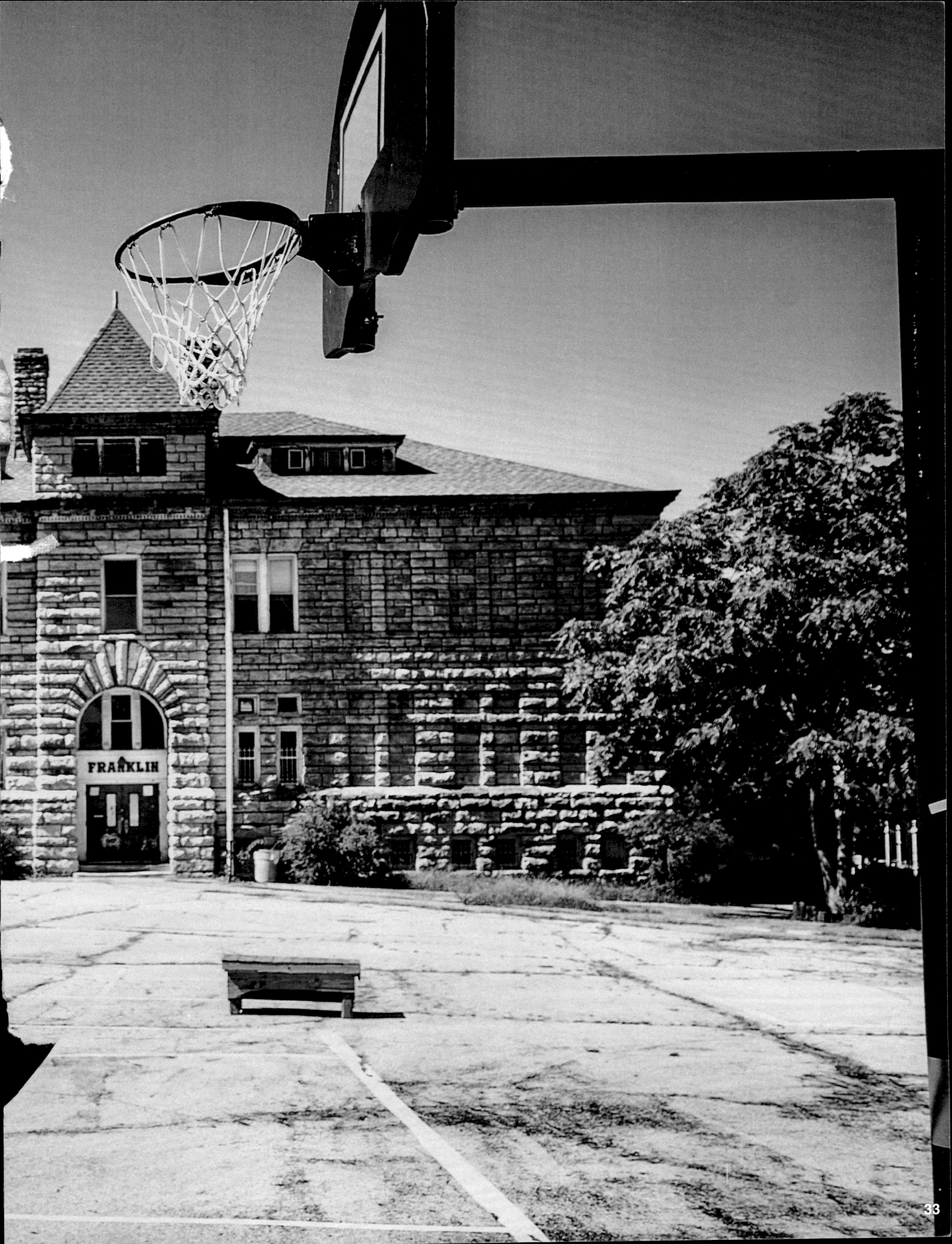
FRANKLIN

HELL JU[ST]
SEEMS B[EST]
FOR ME.

A motherless child is how I feel,
As I walk these roads on my own.
Do you hear my bones rattle in my skin?
Cause they're getting weary of this un-precious fold.

I know how it feels to be in pain
And feel the life drained from my veins.
I'm screaming,
I'm sorry God. I'm sorry.

Show me how I can change.
Show me the path, which you wish for me to follow.
Lord, I just want a sip of success,
But it seems the pain is way too hard to swallow.

I feel like the boy in the spotlight
Out blinded by the darkness.
Hell just seems best for me,
Cause my anger would have the devil hiding in his closet.

Just leave me alone
Or throw me a rope, and tell me come on.
I want to change this pain
To help me gain a chance to keep me sane.

Hush…
Listen to the silenced hearts.
I'm with millions lying in the sun,
But feel like I'm alone in the dark.

Motherless child. ■

I SPEAK MY MIND, BECAUSE I HAVE A VOICE, AND IT MATTERS.

They think that I will follow in their footsteps. They think that I'll be just another stereotype, another young black female pregnant and/or dropping out of school by the age of sixteen. They think that I am naïve still, dumb, incapable of thinking for myself and forming my own opinion. She thinks I'll be just like the rest of them. He thinks I still need to be taught things that he can't even teach me. They think that I am still a child. They think that I am going to fail, that I can't be trusted to make my own decisions, because I fit "that" description. They think that if they tell me "no", I'm just going to stop. They think that I am completely oblivious to their ignorance. They think that I am stuck up and a know-it-all, because I speak my mind. They think that I…me…am a bad child. If only they knew. I speak my mind, because I have a voice, and it matters. I may seem stuck up, but only I truly believe I am above drugs, violence and stupidity, and that is something that I am dang gone proud of. They don't know that if they tell me "no" they won't give me money I need for school activities, or a ride to work, or support and congratulations on my successes that I will still continue to achieve, and I will find the money to pay for those activities. They don't know that no matter how hard they hope and pray and wish that I will fall into that stereotype or follow in their footsteps, I WILL NOT be stuck living pay check to pay check or in the projects on food stamps. I will either succeed or be successful trying. And if they weren't busy being jealous of me, maybe they could take the time to get to know me, and if they knew me, they would know that failure is not an option. ■

My perfect world is when I can go places and wouldn't have to worry about getting killed or seeing someone getting killed. I wanna be able to sleep at night without hearing gunshots. I wish everybody can live forever, because sometimes your loved ones you wouldn't wanna let them go. My perfect world is everybody is peaceful, everybody get along with everybody, because the world be a better place without gangs or violence, but even thou this perfect world isn't here right now, I still pray for it to come. I will never lose hope. ■

I know it seems crazy but sagging is so cute to me. Well it depends on how low the sag is. If it is between the butt and knees than that is so cute, but if it is below the knees that's a turn off, and it's really dusty. The sag of people can really show a lot, like it can say you have a gun. ■

But what I really need is someone to love me. When I look around I don't see it. My mom, oh she hates me, and I hate her. Well I guess our love – it already burned. And my dad, that stranger, he's locked away writing to me every day. I sometimes write back, but my memory is wack, very forgetful. So all those years he was out of my life, it was like he never was there. So I'm use to it by now, so I say I don't care. But it's a lie. I do. I want him by me, beside me, rite in front were I can see the love in his eyes. But it's a tough life, so that rite there never gunna happen, nope. I no he loves me, and that not enough. Every day I just wanna give up. I wish I wasn't so big. I think I ok, but not other kids. I've bin bullyed since I ever could remember, but now I live a life of lies. I say its normall, but its not. I be who they want me to be. I hang out with most. I make my personality wat they want it to be and the truth is knowone knows the reall me, not even me. I think my life is bad, but then I see worst, but in my mind that doesn't matter. I put how I feel in words thinking no one will ever read them and if they do, they won't care. Not there life, problem, pain so why care? Me, I'll tell you a secret, hoping you'll keep it. Look at my arm (left) and you won't believe it. Scarse of anger, I inflict pain on my self no one els. Am I going insane? I guess I'm fine. I tell myself to carry on. I like to write music, express "ME" in a song. My life as child well that was all drugs, thugs, no money, no hugs so wat write? Who cares enyway? Maybe I should get a man to love my pain away? That's what I hope for will always happen, but would it really, truly fix it? ■

A father and a daddy – a father is the authority and discipline. He allows himself to be a part of the family, the leader and the one responsible for all actions. A daddy would be the man who just gave your mother a child. ■

Boredom can take a person down a destructive path. This path can easily lead to influences from the wrong things such as drugs and dropping out of school. Boredom has taken a part in my life where it led me into the wrong crowd of "friends." Boredom led me into believing school wasn't for me. I would always think that positivity was boring, so I did the opposite. ■

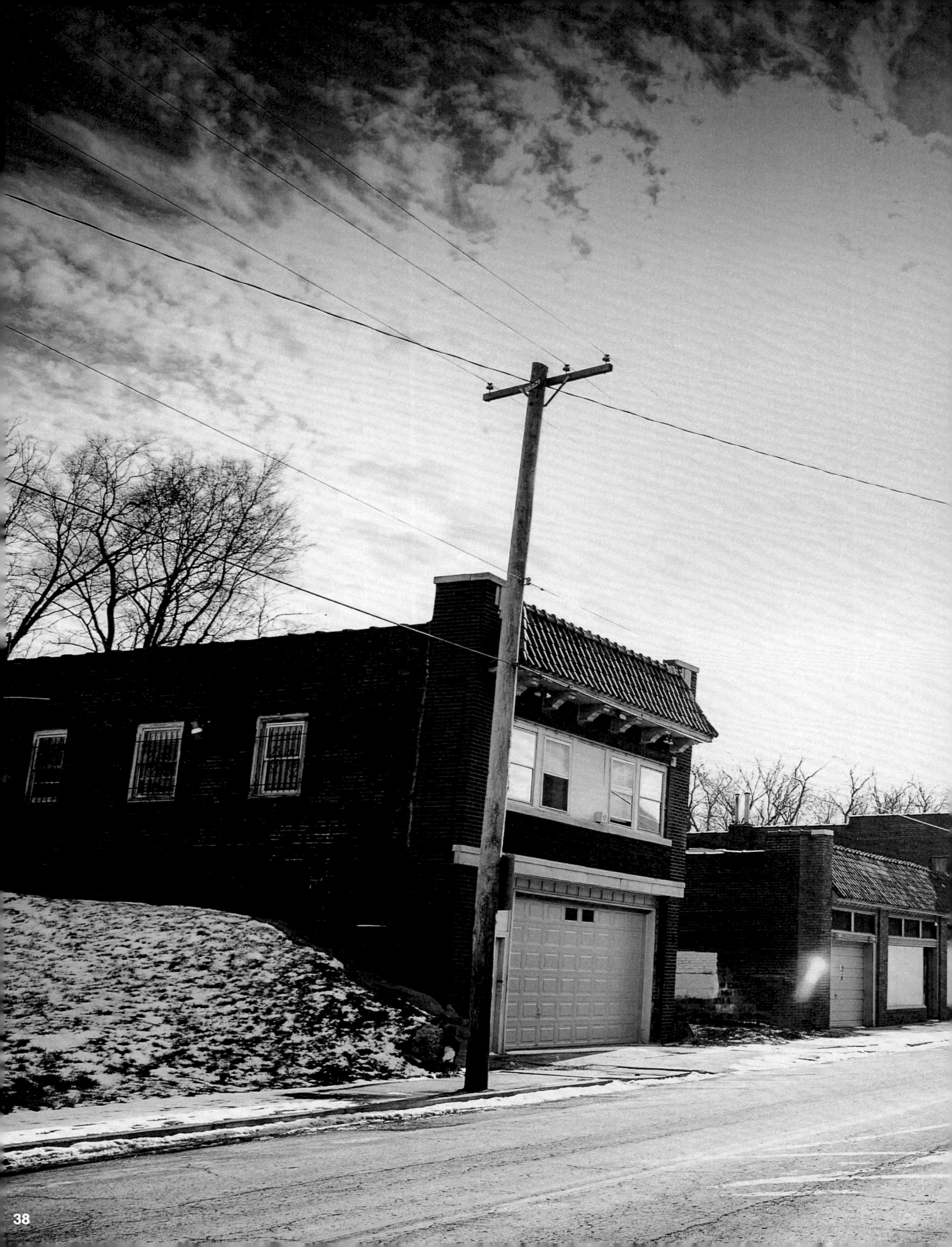

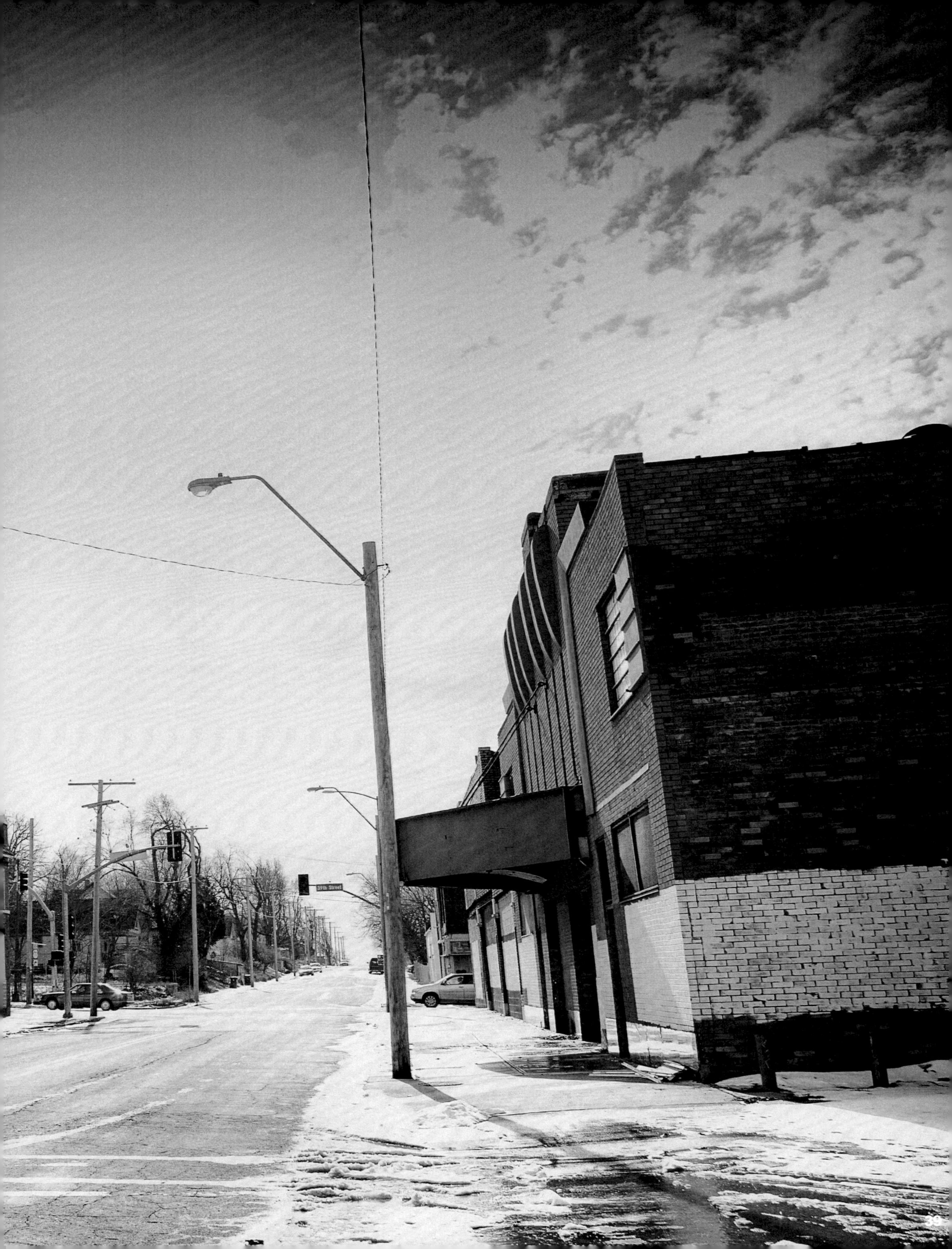
39th Street

THEY DO[
THAT SOM
JUST NEE

I'T KNOW
ETIMES I
DA HUG

4037

Well, at first I was freaking out. I wasn't really scared, but I didn't know what the dad was going to do. I didn't know what he was going to think or say. At first he felt scared, not ready, but now he is ready and happy.

Um, yeah, to this day I'm still pretty freaked out. But at the same time I am happy, 'cause I've always wanted a baby. But not at this age. I'm 14 and too young and still in school. Yeah, I was just worried I was going to be alone on this, but I'm not, because the dad wants the baby and wants to be there. I'm scared of the hospital part, nine months from now, what pain I'ma be in and the needle that they're going to inject in me.

I think Gremlin and Lil Gremlin are changing my life, and I am so very happy, except for the fact that I had to quit everything like play fighting with family and friends, drinking and smoking, especially weed – that is my addiction. But I'll do anything for this baby. The dad is in a group home, and doing better. He's improving and staying out of trouble, 'cause he found out I was pregnant. He's changed now and is going to be there for me and the baby. I am happy and thankful. ■

I am from a place where good values were taught, go to church and get your Jesus on, work hard for what you want to do, cause you're the one you have to live with. Adversity is the hardest to handle. My father wasn't there when I blew out my first candle. He was away at work breaking his back just so us kids could have a good life. Finally re-united, my parents, brother and I came across the border when I was older than five. Without an idea of the language, no house and no job they thought we would collapse, but look at us now. My dad has his own business and mom a beautiful home. The kids? Those poor doubted souls are top of the class and getting running awards. ■

Never have I ever felt worthless. It was taught to me that everyone has a purpose in life. God made me to be full of worth. The feeling of worthlessness is there in the worst of times. When those look down upon you, they are ignorant, because everyone has a talent, a purpose, and worth. The day I feel worthless is the day I will look to God and ask him to remind me of what I am worth. ■

I am from a neighborhood where you're judged by what you wear, brands, sizes and even colors. I come from a neighborhood where there are more buildings closed than there are open. I'm from moving house to house every now and again, because my mom can't make ends on her own. I'm from hurt and forgiveness. I have messed up and hurt people who least deserved it, but I have been blessed to be forgiven and surrounded by people that love me. ■

WE ONLY HAVE THREE DRUG HOUSES ON MY STREET.

"I've only been in two. It sounds weird, but I felt safe."

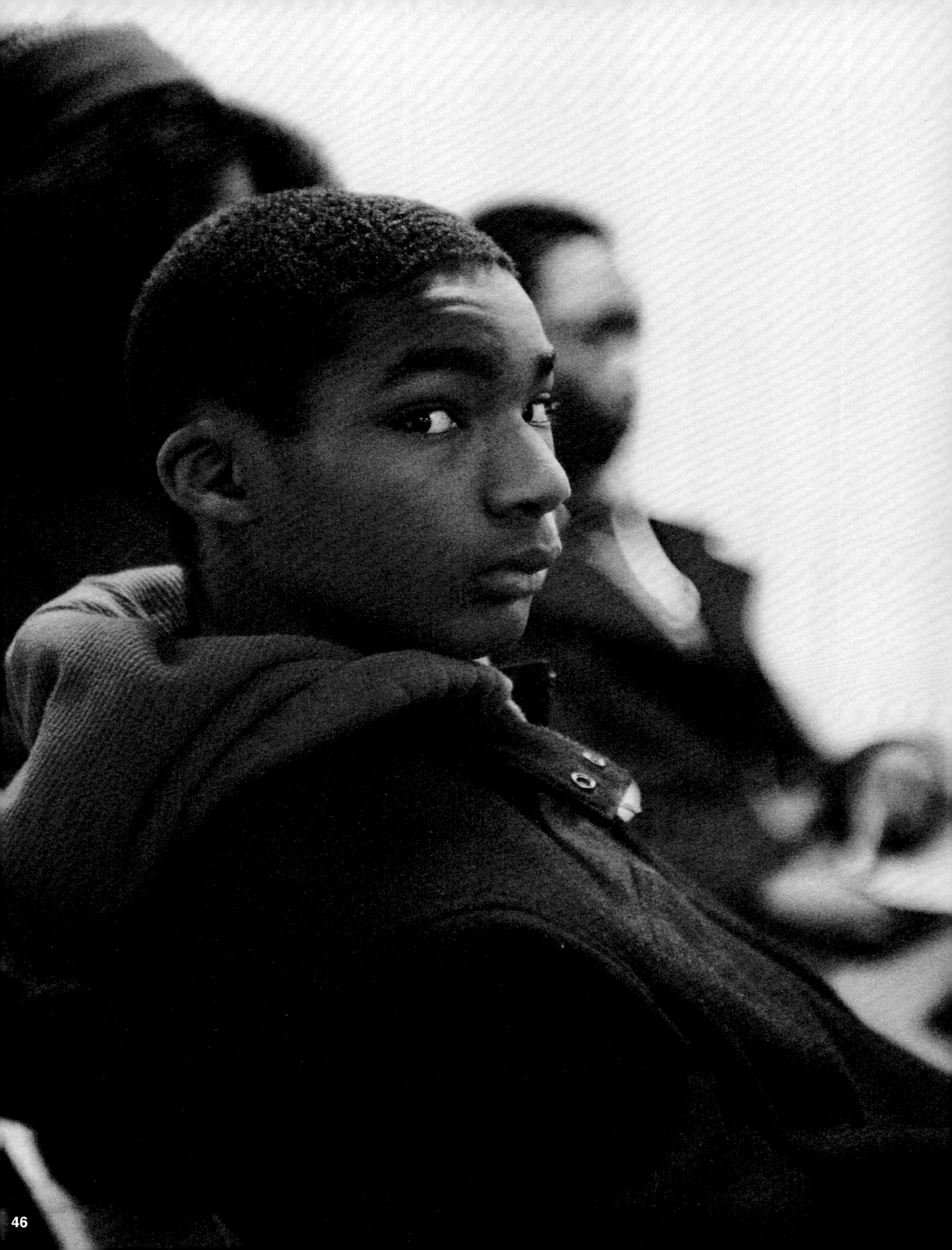

This is one of my friends. He's old, bald headed, tatted with dark brown eyes. He says whatever he has on his mind. Well, this guy inspired me to stop gangbanging. He told me I can do something good and better in life. If I had something to tell him I would tell him, "Thanks for everything. Thanks for having my back." ∎

God empowers me, cause without him I wouldn't want to go on with my day, my life, myself. He picks me up, wakes me up, and keeps me living. He inspires me to believe in myself and makes me feel hope that there is a way. There is a blessing. He answers my prayers and makes me feel powerful. I love that man, my father savior Jesus. ∎

Shorts are getting shorter, pants are getting lower, and all the music involves lyrics filled with nigga this and nigga that. The generation's lingo becomes shorter. The screens are smaller. As time flies by, in my opinion, people become oblivious to their surroundings. Everything changes, especially the rules. It's okay for nine year olds to show their privates off on Facebook. It's expected at age thirteen to have babies in the making. Boys have swag and use "YOLO" at every stupid or embarrassing thing they do. People went from Frank Sinatra and Aerosmith to Wiz Khalifa and Lil' Wayne. Every little kid needs an ipad, 4G phone, and laptop instead of crayons, yoyos and the Bop-its. All I'm trying to say is things change but not always for the best. ∎

I'M SICK OF SEEING YOUNG FOLK DIE BECAUSE OF PETTY THINGS.

I live with my grandma and my great-grandma and my little brother. My brother is 12, and he's so irritating. I know it's because he's my little brother, but he always does stuff to upset me like pee on the seat or something. (My grandma really hates that!) My grandma, she's fun to be around sometimes. She just talks a lot. She's one of those grandmas that likes to tell all the embarrassing childhood stories. My great grandma – she can't walk so good, so we all do our part in looking after her, making sure that she's fed and bathed. We also help her exercise her legs. My great grandma is the nicest person on earth to me. She inspires everyone in my family to just be positive and have faith. She makes everyone's day better with her smile even if she only has four teeth. ■

Today my mama is the lady I live with, but I was not born to her. I was adopted as well as my siblings. It's not a secret, but it's not something everyone knows. In fact, most people think I have the best life. Trust me, I do not. It's not like I am upset with being adopted. All I want is for my biological mom to tell me why she did not want me. Ever since I was little I thought it was because I was a bad kid. And ever since I was little I have kept this to myself. There are countless nights I have cried. But do people care? I really don't think so. They don't ask. Or maybe they don't ask, because they don't know. ■

In fifth grade we had a guest speaker who had a story related to mine, but she said the only reason she was there was because she let go and forgave. After that I did exactly what she told us to do. I also had a conversation with my mama, which really showed me she cared. ■

It's an addiction starting from a cry for attention. I don't want this to sound like I think I have the most heartbreaking story, because if you ask anyone, starving kids in Africa are the only people who are allowed to have problems. "I wanna stay inside all day. I want the world to go away. I want to be a real fake." An attention cry. I wanted to be noticed. I wanted people to know I wasn't happy. I didn't want to be the girl I was. So the only logical thing I thought there was to do was slice my skin open. Cutting proved to be more than a way to subliminally cry for attention and sympathy. I could now transfer my self-hatred from my mind to my skin. So here's to being fat, stupid, unwanted, ugly and worthless. The addiction is starting. People saw. I denied. They commented. I made excuses. I was satisfied. I got what I wanted after years of being ignored. "I love you, baby. You know that. But if you want to stay friends with my daughter you need to stop. I don't want her going to any funerals." This was my best friend's mom. It got me to stop for a couple of months. People crave food. I craved carving my skin. And when I craved food, I carved. You need to be perfect. Getting fat isn't very perfect of you, I thought. I don't know how my self-image got that bad. It started up again. There is so much wrong with my body to begin, then myself. Okay. I started everything over attention, then it got to seeing myself hurt and bleeding. It got worse. This time no one noticed. It turned into an everyday routine. School, sleep, get up at 12am, vitamins, cut, then school again. I was at my worst where I just didn't care anymore. Lose my friends? Cool. Parents don't know what's going on? Alright. Ready to die? Yeah. The scariest thing was thinking about dying and being completely fine with it. Everywhere I'd go I'd look around and think about how I could kill myself there. I'd look over ledges and think if it would kill me if I jumped. I wasn't in control anymore. My disease was. I wanted help. I really did. But with everything else going on my parents would blame themselves. Who wants to know their kid didn't dream of Disneyland like all the others but wanted to die? My mom was hospitalized at the time for an attempted suicide. I wanted to tell her. I really just couldn't. It was my fault, my problem, and I'll find a way out. ■

Life can be perfect, but for me my life isn't near perfect. Everyday is a new day for me, but everyday it's the same old things. As I grew up as a little girl everyday I would see abuse and cruel things. No one knew - just the people that lived in my house. We were all afraid to let a word out. They might of thought I was too little to understand, but I was smart enough to know what was going on. I was just a little girl. I didn't understand what was the meaning of life yet. I didn't know whether what I was seeing with my own eyes was bad or good. But as I grew older I began to start putting pieces together little by little. My mom never told me anything. All she ever tried to do was protect her children. But she never knew I saw things, and I've never told her - still to this day. My mom was abused and everything else that you can't imagine. But when I turned 7, thank God, everything was all over. I'm 16 now. I try not to think of the past, but it's chasing me. It's eating me alive. I try so darn hard to not think of it. When I do I get so angry. So angry! I just cry so much, because of all the anger built up inside of me. And now, because of all the abuse my mom has been through, she is very sick. She is really weak. And all I can blame is my dad. But I hate my dad with a passion. I'm just so angry. I'm angry at the world. I have to live with my mom being sick every single day of my life. But no one knows, not my friends, not my cousins, no one. So I call myself a broken little bird running, flying, trying to find answers just so I can find my way out to be free from all the pain. I would do anything, anything in the world, to see my mom happy again. But all I can do is pray to God and believe that everything will be okay. For now, I'm going to live my life. I'm going to make my mom's dreams that she wants for me come true. I'm going to try my hardest, the hardest I'll ever try in my life. Even if she doesn't make it through to see me achieve it, I'm going to do it for her, for my mom, because it's my motivation. It's my destiny. ∎

YES, EVERYONE KNOWS THE PERSON I AM TODAY, BUT DO THEY CARE ABOUT MY YESTERDAY?

I think there is a lot to change about our generation, so we as teenagers must fight for it, like violence. Now most of you might not care, because it hasn't happened to you yet or anyone in your family, but that's a problem. We have this careless cold-hearted mindset until somebody in our family has been affected personally. I haven't experienced it, but I know it's out there, so we as a people (especially black) must come together and fight for nonviolence. Instead, we sit back and keep our mouths shut and tell each other not to "snitch". If we don't, the cycle will continue, because it's all about revenge. If it was somebody in your family, you would want answers. ∎

I think that I am smrat and that I can do what ever I put my mind to, because she sad to me that over over again, and I really thank my mom for that and what she has said to me when times got bad, and I could not do it by myself. ∎

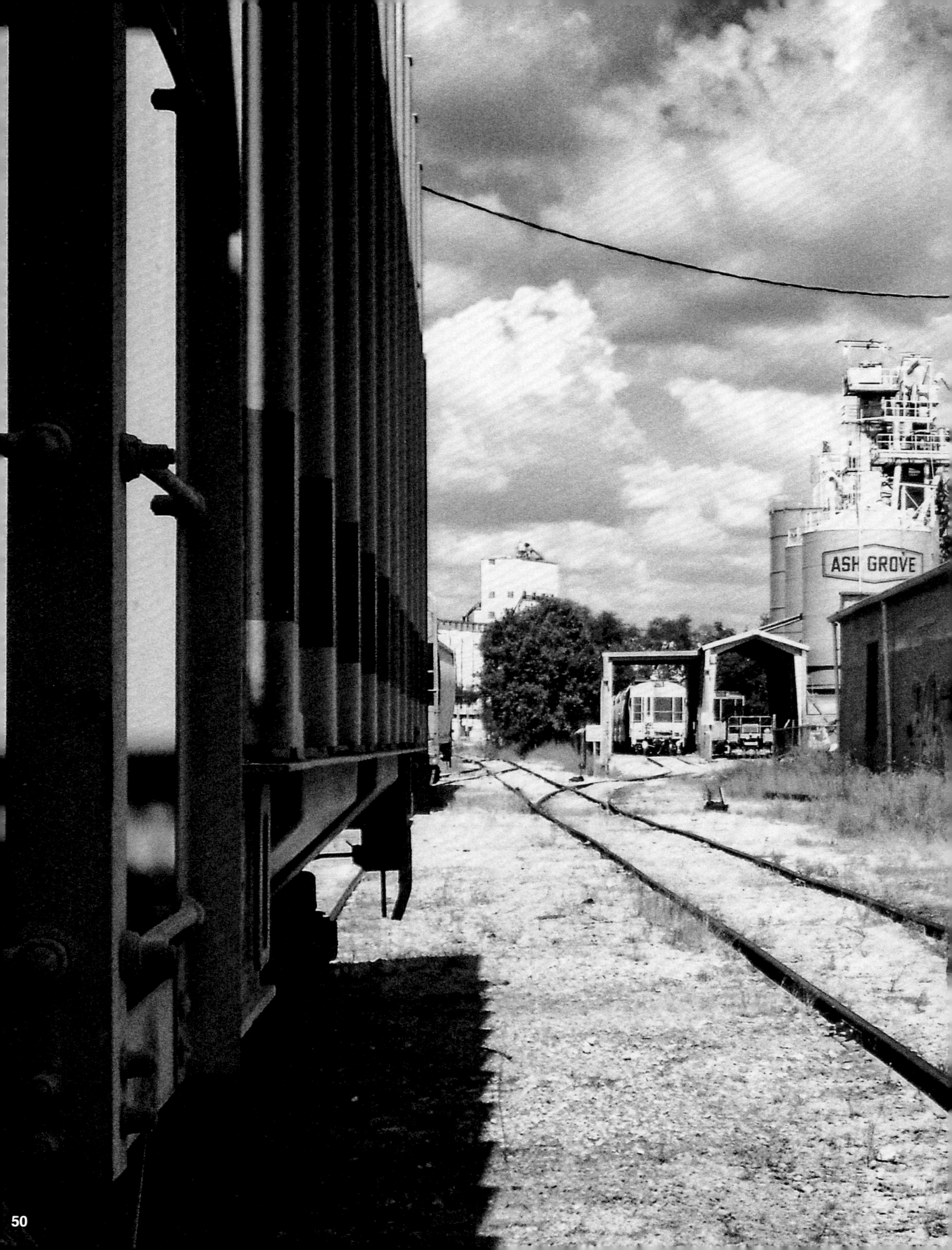
ASH GROVE

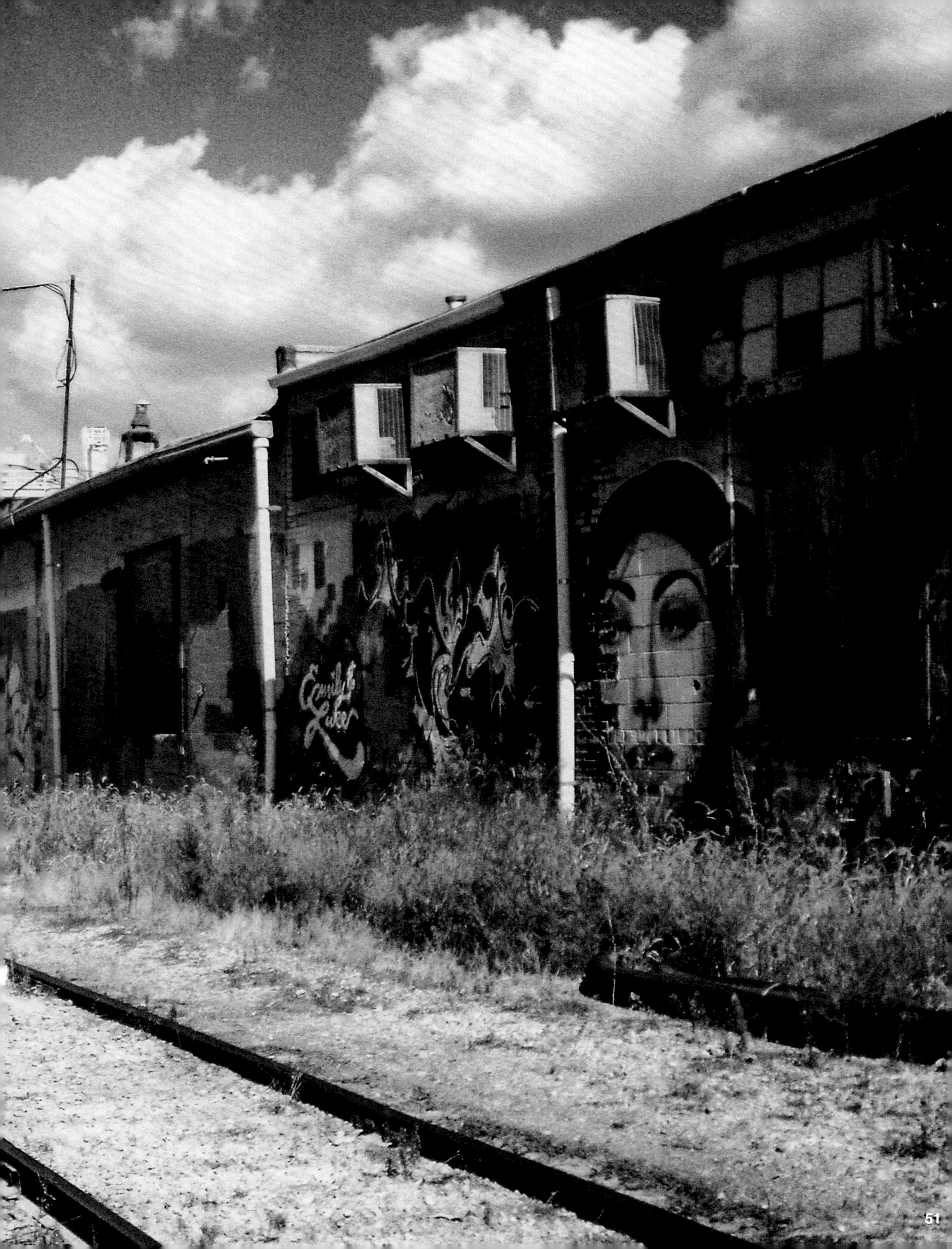

I hope for a better future.
I hope there's a pot of gold at the end of the rainbow.
I hope God will get me through the bad times.
I hope I can help others one day.
In the past I had no hope,
so now that I do, I can achieve more. ∎

THE FACT THAT I AM AN AFRICAN AMERICAN MALE GETS IN THE WAY OF OPPORTUNITIES IN LIFE, BECAUSE RACISM IS SO TOUGH. IT STOPS ME FROM HAVING THE THINGS THAT A BOY MY AGE SHOULD HAVE LIKE A JOB. I HAVE TO WONDER WHY.

Snitching – You think that shit is cool – keep your mouth shut when stuff go down? You think you gain respect by shutting up? Well instead of snitching high and alert, in your hood you better dumb it down and stand up and speak ya mind. Cuz if you don't like what's going down, open ya mouth. Cuz, if you do it too late, then another life is lost, and you could've stopped it. Now you feel guilty. So, get this advice from me and stand tall and open up. Tell ya homies, "Look that shit ain't cool." Cuz once one of your family members lie dead on yo block before ya eyes, I know you want answers. But yo homies like, "we don't snitch round here," and now you stuck and lost, cuz you can't get answers. Well, stand up, don't be a lil punk, and let yo voice be heard. I know mine was. ∎

We should be fighting for that kids can make a different and that just because on kid missit up don't mean we are all misst up. We can help one and a nother. That their should be more man in house holds to day not in jail but with they kids. ■

I am from the big white house on the corner of Jackson where the only grocery store around is Happy Foods – a store where it's name says absolutely nothing about the products nor quality of the store. I am from a black family who opens up our home to anybody, despite the untrustworthy people who linger around the ally at night. I am from a series of gunshots at night, and as I lie in my bed every single night, I'm saddened to know that I've become immune to hearing the glock pop off nearby. I am from Christianity every Sunday morning. I am from the Baptist church on 27th and Wabash. I am from prayer and faith that oftentimes becomes a shield, not only on my neighborhood, but my life. ■

Okay, there is always going to be something that holds me back, like getting pregnant, but I will tell you this: I won't ever regret my baby. God gave me a gift for a reason and can take it just like nothing. That's where I have to be careful and try to change my life. I'm going to try, but something's always pulling my back. Besides a baby holding you back, there are bigger things that are worse than that – like losing everybody. Or at least that's what it feels like. I'm only 14 and already I have lost like 7 or 8 people as the years go by to violence. There's that and gangs, and your dad beating your mom in front of you, or the welfare always up your ass trying to tear your family apart, or always being in jail or on house arrest or probation. ■

Equality is what our previous generation fought for. It often seems as if their efforts went to waste because of the way we treat each other. Our generation should focus our efforts on unity. There are so many people in the world from different ethnic backgrounds with different religions and beliefs. However, we are all people. Stick up together should be a priority. If everyone stuck together and helped one another out, there would be less homelessness, murders and suicides. We are better as a group than alone. The faster people realize this, the better off we all will be as a nation. ■

I may say sticks 'n stones may break my bones but words will never hurt me. Lied! Yep that is a lie. Your words are the switches that my slave master uses. See your words leave marks -marks that will take years to clean. I'm afraid to say how I feel, because I don't want to hurt you. But the more I keep quiet the more those switches feel like bullets, bullets that keep killing me … those switches aren't for me or anyone else. They're for a cow or horse, and I'm not an animal. ■

My biggest fear is that people will fined out that I can't read. I will be so mad if someone did find out about cause then I will feel like they are take avaniech over me. They will make me read stuff out loud are make fun of me then I really don't want to go back to school cause mrs dent make you read everything out loud. I am every every scared out that. They know that I can't read from last year cause we always had to read out loud. ■

> *MY BIGGEST FEAR IS THUNDER, BUT NOT BECAUSE IT IS LOUD. THE SOUND FRIGHTENS ME, BUT I'M AFRAID THAT IT WILL STRIKE ME DOWN FOR ALL THE WRONG I'VE DONE.*

During my eighth grade year I was going to Southwest. I was being a little wild and my grades started to drop. My family started to come up to my school, groups at a time. They sat in my classes with me. At the time it was embarrassing, but at the end of the school year my grades went up and I passed. ∎

Maybe I just hold too much in, and it's my turn for God to put my tears in a bottle, so that I will feel relieved. ∎

My biggest fear in life is being a failure and disappointment to my parents. I want to be a successful woman and change the definition of a hard working African American woman. My parents have put so much time, effort and money to better my education, and I would like to repay them with my own success. ∎

I like being black, because it symbolizes that I am proud. People expect me to be ghetto and uneducated, so are shocked when they find out I'm a 10th grader testing on a 12th grade level for reading and about 12th grade for math. It just shows – don't judge a book by its cover. ∎

I am from the respect and protectiveness of the hustlers, dealers and those I call neighbor, the prostitutes, drug-addicts and criminals that walk the street of Prospect where there is a shoot-out at least once a week, from the teenagers that walk around like they K.C. without a parent to tell them otherwise. I am from the girl down the street getting pregnant before midterms, from the judgment of others that don't understand the struggle I've been through and continue to go through each day. I am from Seattle, Atlanta and Kansas City, from a kicked in door by the friends my mother associated herself with, from making good grades to failing within two years. I am from the screams of mothers, fathers and siblings as they learn their child is gone, from a room full of people all there to celebrate the life of a loved one that didn't get to see a new day, from the death of a friend, classmate and family member. ∎

It's something I can't explain. It's a feeling - dying before no one can hear, drowning in my depression - my emotions are not there. My thoughts in a compressor chopped up, cut short, breathless, panting, my heart is distant, broken. No glue could put my pieces back together. No feet could walk in my steps, because my biggest fear is fearing anything. ∎

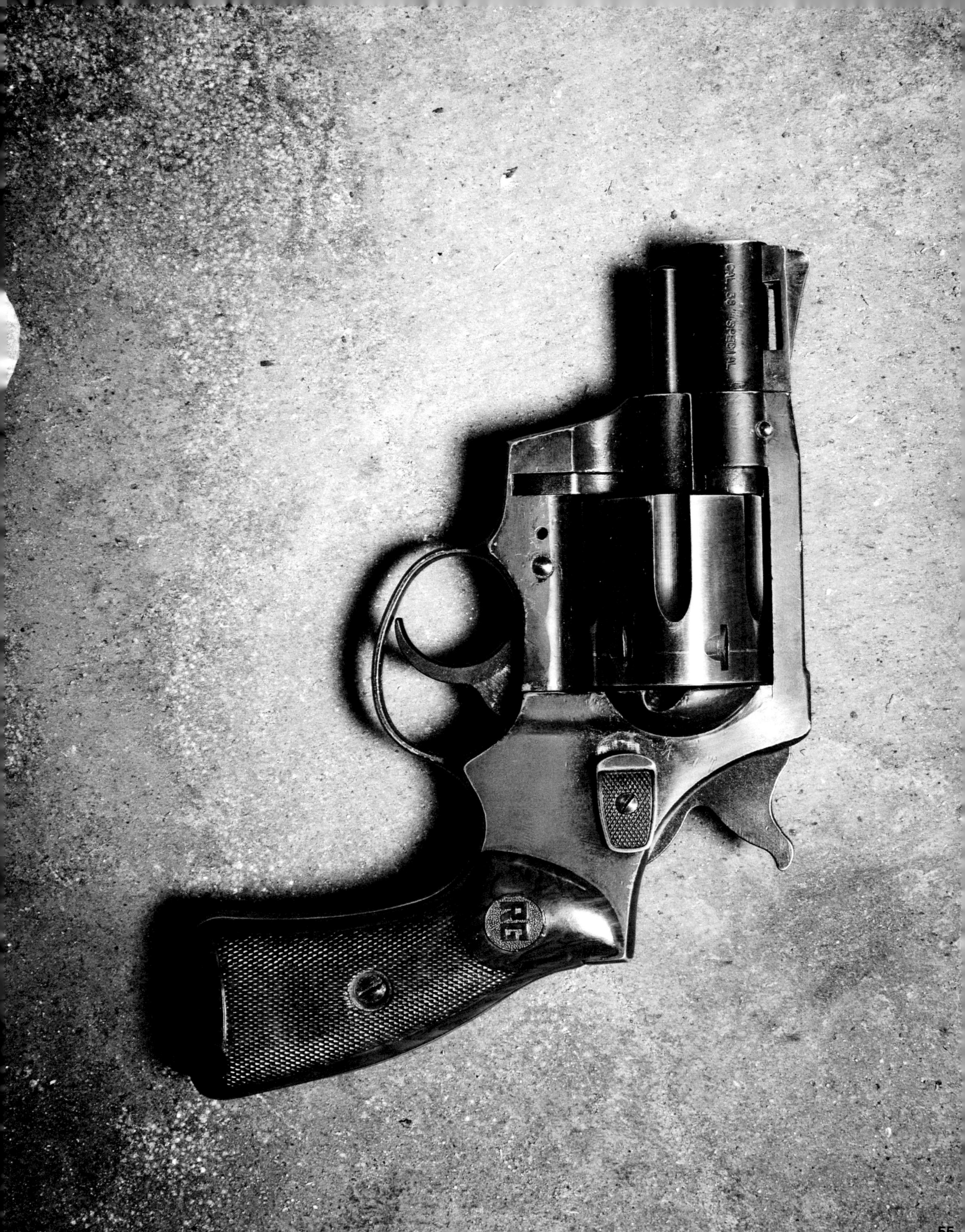

HE HELD A GUN TO MY FACE.

MY HEART RACED.

When I lived with my mom I was four when I started sleeping in a chair. I slept well in the chair, but there wasn't that much room to move in it, so I would lose some sleep. I wouldn't care, because I had a TV to watch. I was sleeping in a chair until I was 8 years old.

Then I got stuck in a group home called Gillis. Gillis was nice, but their beds were terrible. The bed frame was made out of metal and the mattress was half the thickness of regular beds. You had to share rooms. I didn't sleep that much, because I didn't trust my roommate. I left Gillis at the age of twelve.

Then I was placed in a foster home. The parents there are really nice. It's just their kids that I hate, because they want me to do stuff for them. My room is on the third floor. It feels good in the winter, but it's hot in the summer. My bed is really soft, and I get enough sleep in my bed. I have lived in this house for over four years, and I'm still living in this house. ∎

If your pants are at the middle of your legs I feel sorry for you, because in jail it means you're someone's nighttime play toy. I feel that most people, mostly black people, should just pull them up. Life would go better for them. Every race does it. It's just 80% Black, so when you think of it, Black people come to mind. I do wish that it would change, so more of us could get better jobs and go more places without getting looked down on. ∎

THE ONLY THING THAT MAKES ME SAD IS HOW LONG IT'S GOING TO TAKE IN ORDER TO GET ADOPTED.

It's always ok to be different and outside the box. I'm different on the outside, but inside is a nice, sweet and friendly person. I stick out, because of what I wear on my head, but it's me. It's what I represent, and if others don't like it, oh well, I was not put on this earth to impress you. It's ok to be yourself and not what everyone else wants you to be. What I wear is just part of what I believe in which is Islam. Appearance is important in my religion, because you don't want to go around showing off your body. It attracts unwanted attention. It's important not to attract unwanted

59

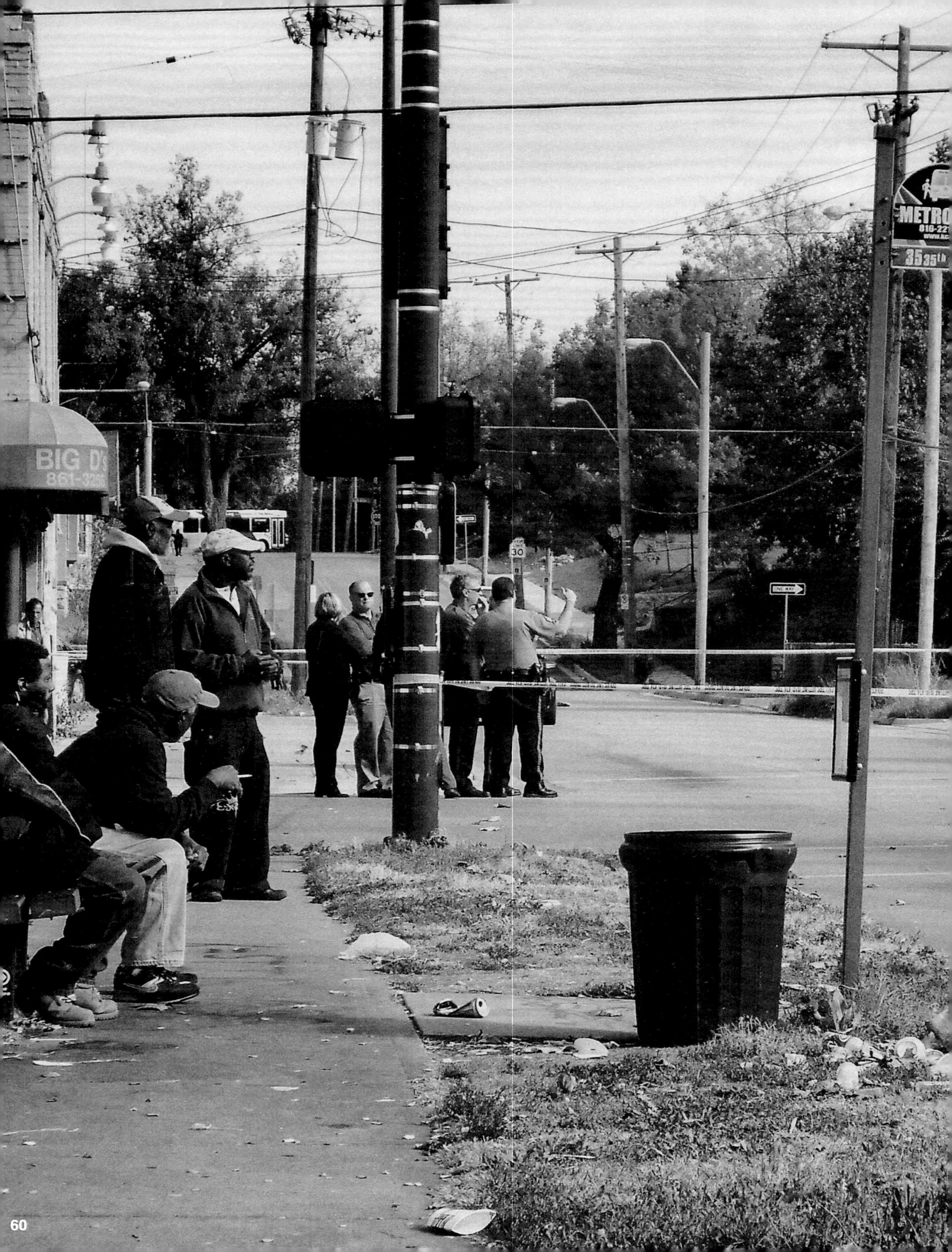
BIG D'S
30
ONE WAY

I'm a hard worker and a dropout. I'm a Mexican basketball player who loves to throw the football. I'm a fatherless father figure to my 11 year old brother. I drink peach Vess and eat jalapeno burgers at Burgers to Go. ■

He held a gun to my face. My heart raced. Pray to God? That's not the case. Middle of winter and swet rolled down my face. My brain stoped and relized all emotions needed to be erased. He asked me what I claimed. What the Hell am I supos to say? My name? I told him to go ahead, and no, I promised him I wouldn't hold him to it. He looked at me as if I was insane, that croked look as though he didn't no what I was saying. I walk closer to the gun saying, "If you were gunna do it, it would already be done. " I looked into his eye – not a tear in my eye, but it looked as if he was gunna cry. He lowerd the gun, and it felt like 1,000 pounds were lifted off of me. He said, "You no what I claim? I claim Forencia 13, but gurl you needa stay off the streets. Your pretty tough from what I see, but were I am aint the best place to be." He walked off with his gun. ■

It was second semester. I was in the sixth grade going into seventh when I started to gang-bang. When getting into a gang, you got to be "jumped" in for 30 seconds, and then you meet the family. I didn't know I was in a gang, because we were like a family, taking care of each other, working out our problems. It is kind of hard trying to make a name for your self. Mine was Nino. It still is, cuz I act like a kid. I had respect, cuz I treated my Homies like my brothers. When they needed something I would always give it to them. A lot of people feared me, cuz I was big and buff. I was the crazy one. I was the crazy one, cuz I was the one that didn't give a fuck. Getting angry is powerful. It was something I was good at. I was feared and respected.

Every day is survival of the fittest. Everywhere you go you have to keep your eyes peeled, even if you're fucked up, for their fools going to pop at you, shoot at you, or do something. One day at Argentine Middle School a new kid came to school, so I was sent to check him. He said something and dissed my hood. I wasn't going to let this pussy do that, so I told him to meet me in the restroom. I kicked his ass bad, like really bad. He called his uncle. He was an O.G. from a rival gang, and he set me up to kill me. I called my girl to tell her my last words, and she was crying. She told me, "I don't want you to die. I don't want you to leave school." I didn't listen. I walked to the alley where they set me up, and the uncle pulled out a gun. Luckily, my friend saw me and hurried up and picked me up before I got shot. Nothing happened thank God, but my heart got broken that day; my girlfriend broke up with me because of what happened. This day I will never forget. ■

The thing that I love about myself is that I am sometime out going. What I mean about that is I care about what other people thing about me...is that I am scared that people will find out about me. I am scarede that people may fined out that I was rape at a youn age. I am scared that people my frind out that I can't really read are spell to good. It hurt me so much that I can't do them things. It hurt me when I was builled at my old school when I was little. It hurt me that I have a learning distablet and that I can't trut in no body, but I want to trut in people, but I just can't do it by myself, and I know I need help, but I am to scared to ask for it. It just hurts me. I try my best to had it all in , but it is to much for me to holde. I can't just always keep it all ball up in side of me know more. That is why I don't smill, but when I do it's just a fake one. I don't smill cause I am hurt. I don't simill coose so much bad stuff have happened to, and never nothing good ever happened to me. I hate when people think that kids have it good. That everything in your life is just all good. Will they are wrong, and I can tell you that for my point of vewe that not everything is good cause it's not. ■

Why cry? All I see is weakness. When I cry I feel the hate and pain coming through my eyes. The tears burn as they fall down my face. I fight the tears, trying to not look weak. When finally one falls, I brush it away and hide my face from others. The thought of being seen makes me hate the tears more. Why must my eyes show my pain when I wish for no one to know? ■

I know this lady that said she was going to change something in her life. I don't think she can change, because she's addicted to it. It's like she needs it in the morning, evening, and at night. When she don't have it, she is a little cranky and itchy. But when she does, she is still kinda itchy but more relaxed and chilled. So overall, I don't think she can change, cause she is immune to it. ■

Depression is a killer. It wraps up its arms around you filling your head with lies. Then it slowly tightens its grip to make you lose your life more and more – the silent killer. So before you put that gun to your head or pop those pills, think about this – Is it worth it? Worth giving the depression the satisfaction of taking your life and trapping your soul? Or will you save yourself and get help? Just know that I was here. Here to talk, listen and to help. Here to be a friend. ■

We are killing our own people. How many of our own have to die until we realize what's going on. Being in a gang may be cool at first, but it is what is turning us against each other. Gangs are the reason my brother and Homies get jumped. Gangs are the reason my Homies get shot or die.

Society is the reason my Homies are in gangs. It starts at school or in the neighborhood. They get in gangs to feel like they belong or to be part of the "familia." If it wasn't for gangs my homeboy would still be alive. If he wasn't in a gang he wouldn't feel the need to have a loaded gun for protection. Ironically, it's what killed him.

I don't like gangs, but I'm still friends with the people in them, or at least some of them. It's funny how my brother doesn't want me to be in a gang, because he thinks it's stupid or I'm stupid for wanting to be in one. Then again, he himself is in a gang. The reason he is still in a gang is because he can't get out. The only way out is death.

I've lost so many homeboys to gang violence that I can't count. How many more funerals do I have to go to? We kill one of theirs. They kill one of ours. It's a never-ending cycle. ■

WE KILL ONE OF THEIRS. THEY KILL ONE OF OURS. IT'S A NEVER-ENDING CYCLE.

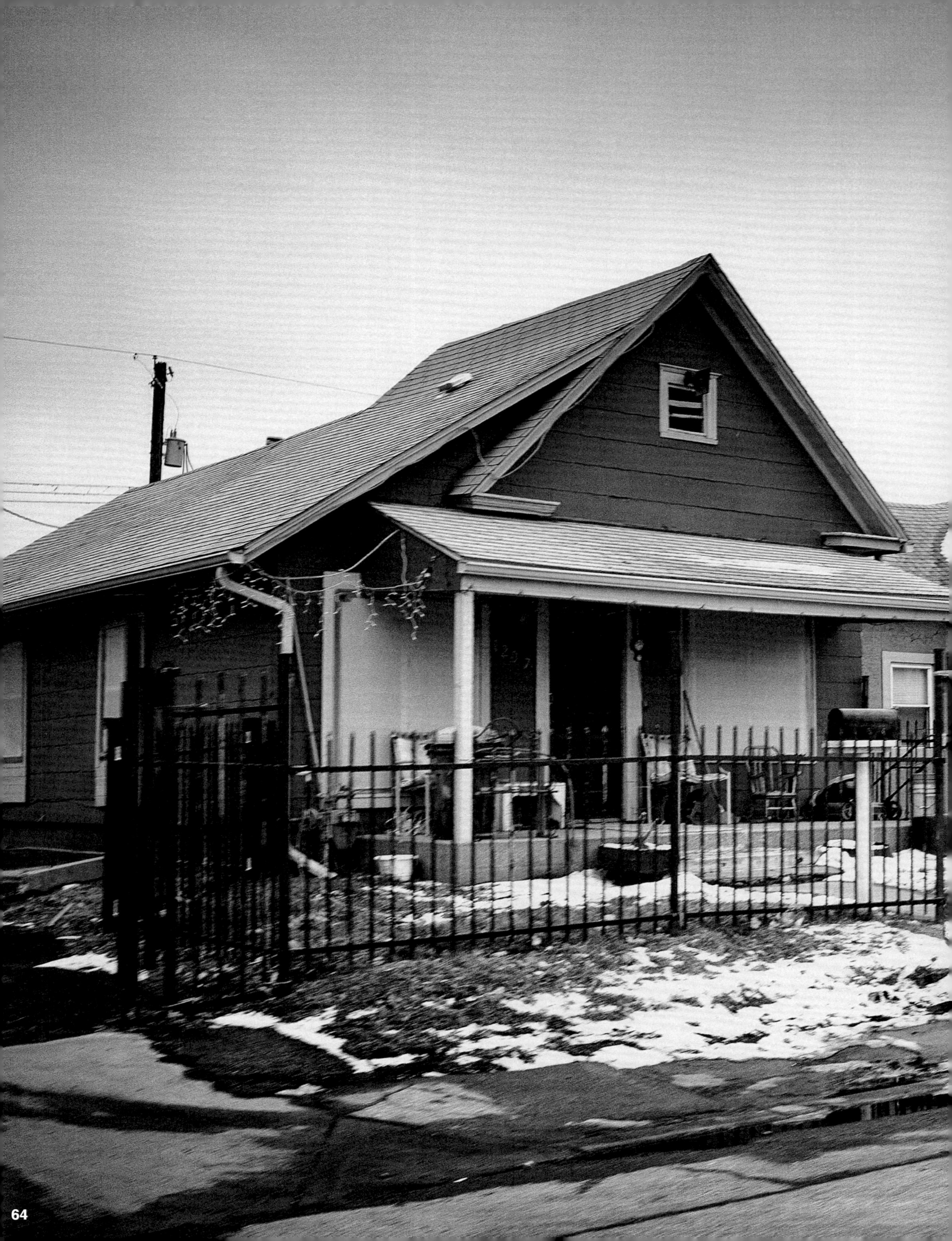

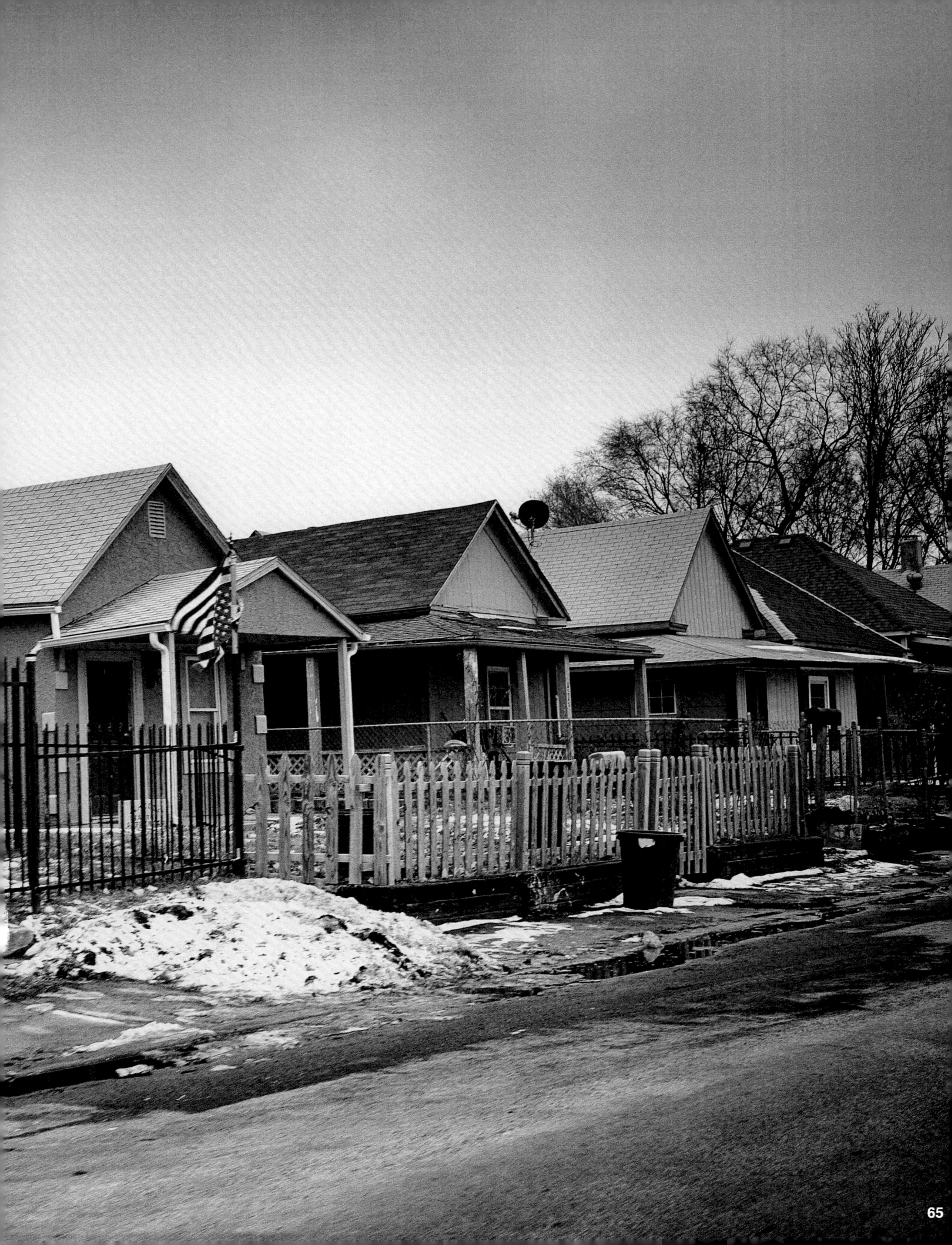

I HAVE TRUST ISSUES AND AM GENERALLY CHARACTERIZED AS ALOOF AND COLD, BUT I'M JUST SCARED.

Dear Dad,

I never saw you except twice, but I never knew it was you. Mom always told me how you were an ass and always on drugs. Why do you never come see me? It really hurts that I don't know my own dad. Auntie always told me that you kept going to jail. Everyone agreed. No one will tell me anything about you. Mom swears you're a bad person, only because you "do" drugs and drink, but also threatened me, mom, and my aunt and her kids. I hate not knowing who you are or how you act like. Only thing I got is a picture of you to go by. Please see me. Everyone knows both parents. Me… well, I'm just bummed, cause they ask me what's your dad like? What does he do? My answer…I don't know who my dad is. That's what gets me, and it hurts to not know.

Love,
Your Daughter.

Dear Uncle,

You have known me since I was a baby - all the good times we shared together. Man looking back, it felt so long ago, like the fourth of July when I was six years old. Man those were some good times.

I remember the time you came to live with me and my family when my dad went missing, because he was on drugs. You never gave up on my dad. You always said he was a good man.

After my father kicked the drug problem he had, he put most of this resentment towards you. He blamed you for his drug problem for some reason. I never did ever get to say goodbye, because your fight was when I was in 3rd or 4th grade. Then I found out you got shot in the head. I remember I found that out in 5th grade. That was the first time I cried for a real reason. So this is my final goodbye from me to you.

Your Friend and Somewhat Nephew.

Dear You,

I heard what you are going through. I want to let you know that I am here for you, and you will never be alone. Don't let these small obstacles in life draw out the map for your life. You say you are being bullied. Not what I think as normal bullied, but bullied by you. And all because of your self-image. You think that you are not beautiful and that you need to look like the girls in the magazine. Well, I'm telling you, you are beautiful. It's not always about the outer beauty but the inner. ■

Dear You,

Why did you leave? Why did you leave my family in two pieces? Why did you decide to start something you couldn't finish? Us. You left your children. You left my mother. You left us. I go through life not being able to ever fully trust someone. I see an apple – I think it's poisoned. I fall in love with a boy – I know he's going to leave. I go through life afraid of what can happen. You wonder why I didn't write "Dear Dad". That's not a title you deserve. It's a title filled with love and confidence. Your kids used to wonder when daddy was coming home. Now you have a new family to raise, and your old one you try to forget. ■

Dear Dropout,

Being uneducated doesn't make you a dropout. Being a dropout makes you uneducated. "Dropout" is nothing but another label the world gives you. My family has a long history of dropouts, so I have a good understanding of what it's like being one; moving from house to house to house, working a dead-end job after dead-end job, not knowing what's for breakfast, lunch or dinner, trying to make it another day without lights. ■

Dear Generation,

Peer pressure can be good and bad. Try to use good peer pressure on our peers, so we can grow up and represent 2016 properly. Also, there is bad peer pressure, and that's okay to be peer pressured, but don't kill nobody. Just don't kill nobody. Seriously, don't kill nobody, because that's not even peer pressure any more. You're just stupid enough to kill somebody. So don't do it. ■

IT ALL START
A LITTLE CU
STARTING TO
AND TRYING
WHAT THEY
WANTED FR

ED WITH
IOSITY,
LIKE BOYS
O SEE
CTUALLY
M ME.

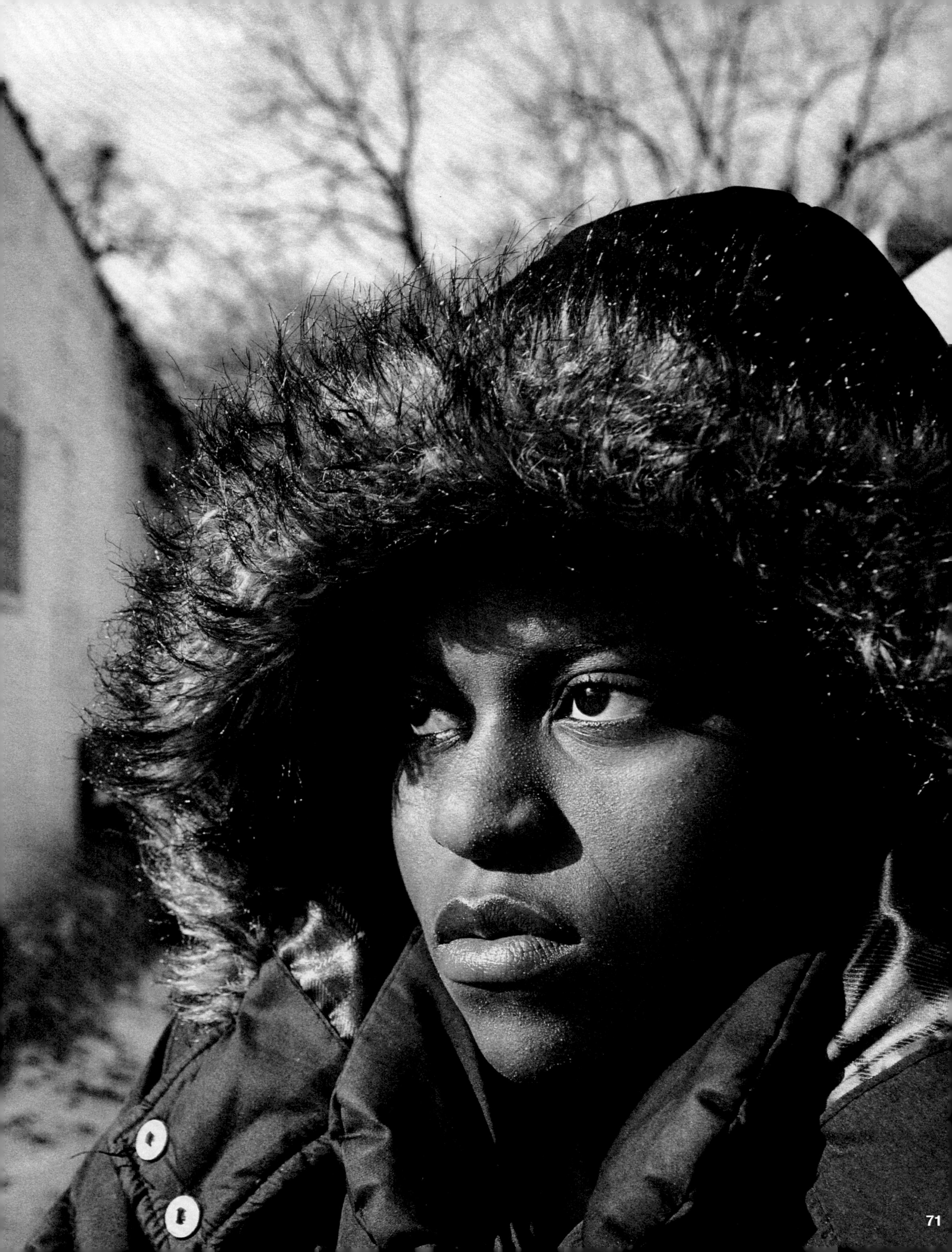

We know what is right,
But we are compelled to do wrong.
Is it instinctual for us to deny
Our instinct of what right and wrong is?
I have a feeling
That the reason we do wrong
Is because we enjoy the pain, or
Can we just not live without it? ■

As I walk down the dark lonely hallway
I hear your voice calling my name.
My heart stops at the sight of your angle face,
Because here I stand getting a view -
One I thought I'd never get again.
My heart aches for you,
So I run into your arms,
But I fall through you.
It was my hopes and imagination,
Hoping you'd return to me,
But I know that the only way I can be with you
Is if I walk through the golden gates in the sky.
Then and there I'll be in your arms. ■

Don't be like your parents or siblings -
Do something with your life.
Don't be like your siblings -
In and out of jail, on the streets, or using drugs.
That's not a way to live.
Don't be like your parents -
Actually finish college.
Get a good job, so you don't have
to be struggling or tryna make ends meet.
Be there for your kids -
Actually love and care about them.
Be yourself -
Don't let others influence you
Into doing the wrong thing.
Don't be like your parents or siblings. ■

I had a dream one day.
It wasn't a long dream.
It wasn't a short dream.
It wasn't a daydream.
In that dream
It had me.
It had things,
A lot of things,
Things I wanted,
Some things I needed,
Gold chains,
Purple planes,
Flat screens.
By any means
It wasn't a lucid dream,
But I controlled these things.
It was hard to figure what my
dream was about.
Then again I found out.
I couldn't believe
It wasn't about me.
It was about vanity. ■

Her soul is gone.
It was stolen by time.
When you look in her eyes
You see nothing –
Just an empty void.
She shows no emotions
Just a blank expression.
They say she's soul less.
I see through the curtain of lies.
She's hiding,
Hiding from this cruel world.
She's in a deep, dark hole,
Waiting for someone to come and
Save her from it.
So I don't understand
Why my love won't reach her. ■

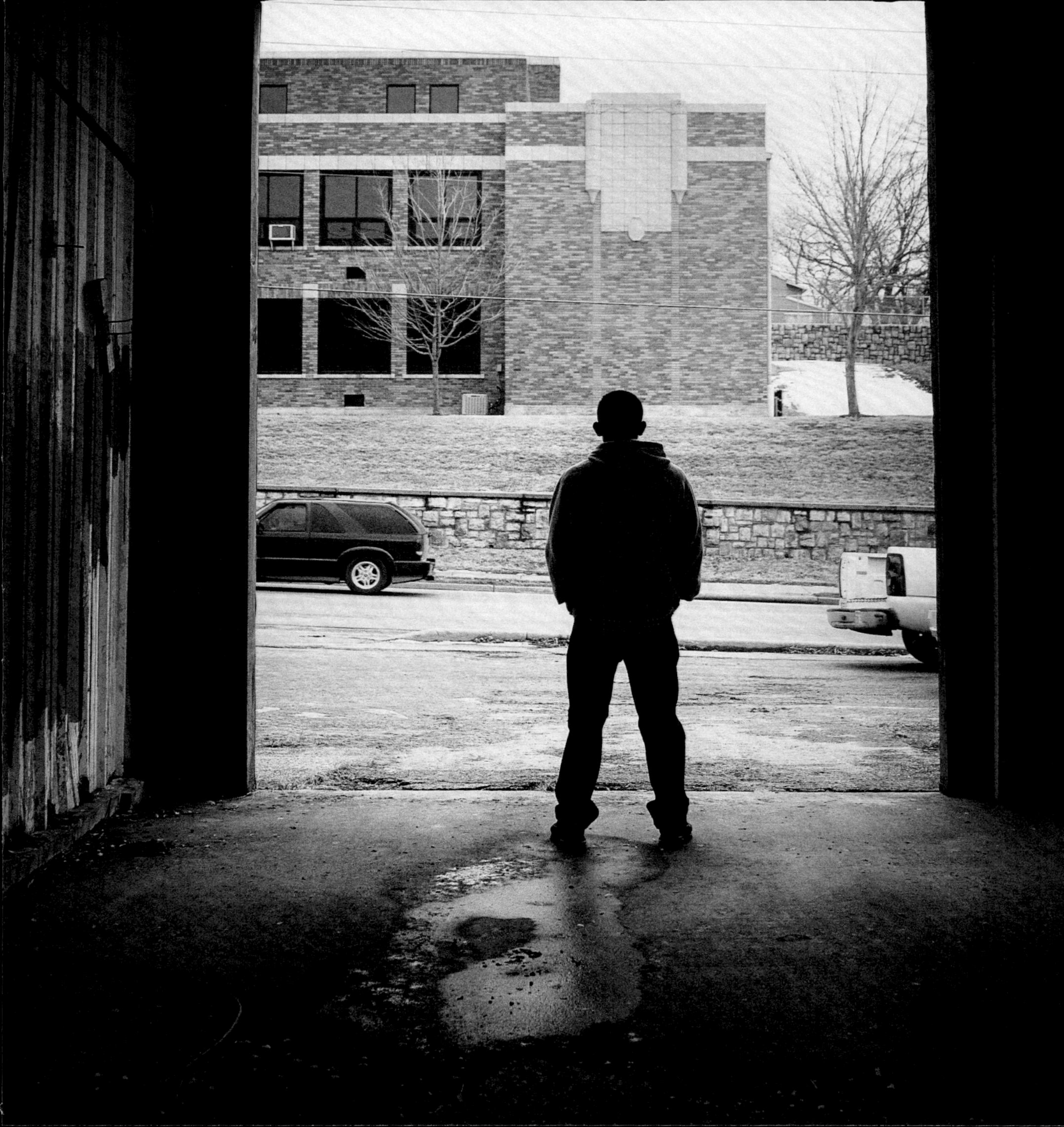

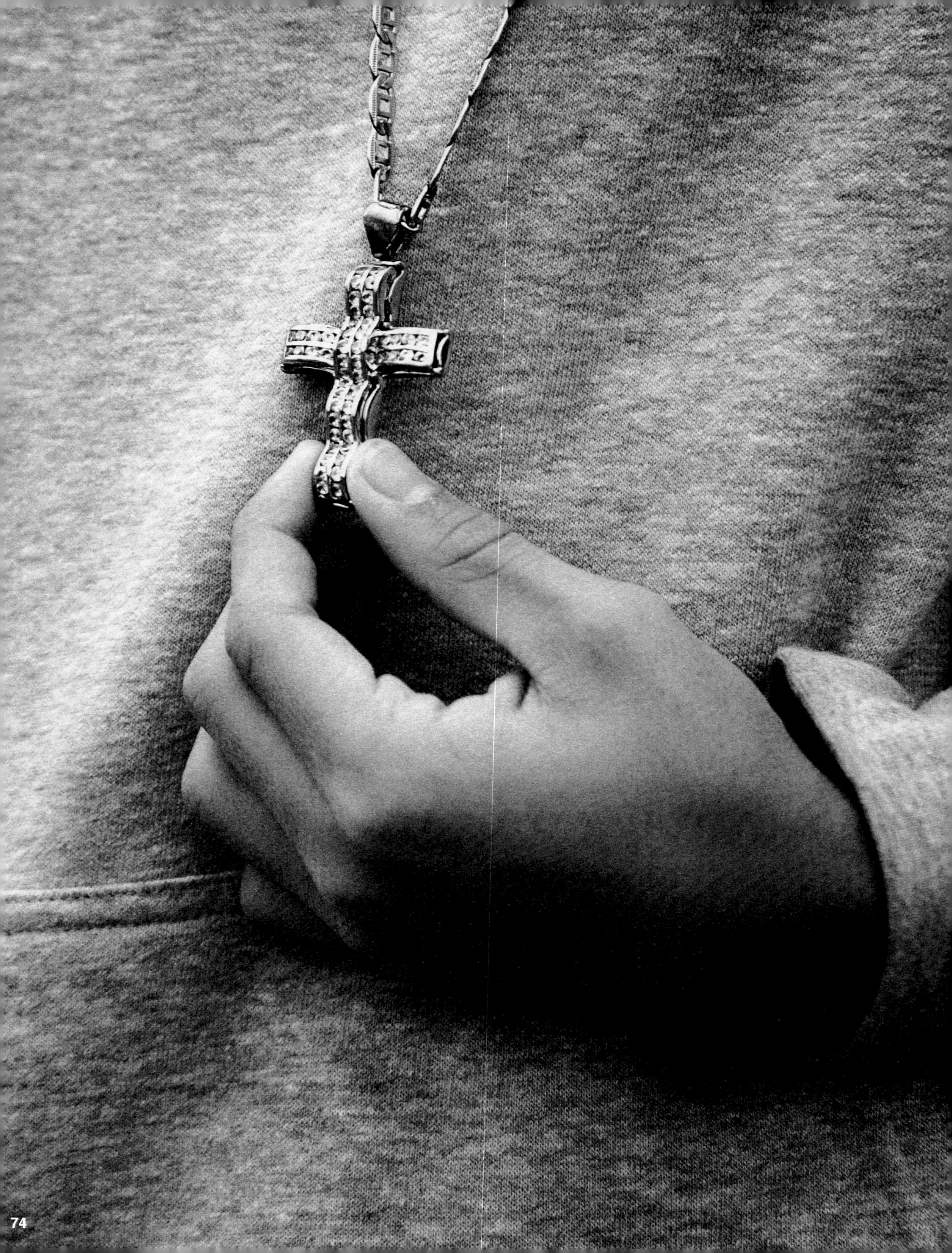

Dear Friend,

How many time I gotta tell you that these boys are just going to use you and try to make you feel dumb and less about yourself? If you want to be loved that badly, I am here to love you as a friend. You can come to me whenever you need. I love you girl. I do wanna see you out here doing anything moving. In the functions, you're shaking your ass, because you think it's cute and okay to be doing. You say you wanna go to college right? Well, let's get into some of these programs to motivate us to go. I really do just want to see you happy and doing well for yourself. These boys won't do it, so I just want to help you do it!

Signed,
Someone Who Cares About You

If life gave a person a chance to start over that would be the day that I want to live through. I know in my life I made a bunch of mistakes, but yet I see myself doing them over and over again. ■

I don't think people truly understand what it is like to be depressed. Or perhaps it's just different for each person. Either way, it's hard to tell.

My depression is like being chained to a wall, heavy burning shackles on each limb. A glass of water that's just out of reach, my head and heart starving, gasping for something. If I were to reach out for the glass, a cruel whip will come down upon me like a terrible crossbreed of thunder and lightening. So I learn to huddle against the chilly and lonely corners of my cell, my mind a slave.

Yet I enjoy touching and being touched. If I were to flinch away or not return a hug, it is only that I am confused and alarmed. Who would want to touch me? An odd, fat girl that couldn't speak up for herself even if she tried. A lonely miserable girl chained to an invisible wall with invisible chains. This does not mean I do not like being hugged.

One day, after a startlingly eventful day at school, I found myself in the pristine white confines of my bathroom, a simple steak knife in my hand. I stared at myself in the mirror long and hard, before I sat on the lidded white toilet and brought the blade onto my upper arm. It was not until then that I started crying. Hot and salty tears fell onto my arm, my trousers, and the white tile.

I did not stop until the pain went away; after the third one the cutting stopped hurting. I have five scars. I did not cut the tender flesh of my underarm where the blue of my veins cover my arm. I was too afraid. Afraid to die maybe. I'm not sure. Perhaps I'm just a coward. I tell that to myself a lot. Anyway, like I said earlier, depression must be different for everyone. I wonder if someone feels shackled like I do? Somehow I doubt it. ■

I actually like my neighborhood despite the way it looks or the things that happen. I like that I have family all around. If anything was to happen I know where to go and how to get there. I also like the people. A lot of the people on my street or my grandma street are real nice. They are all very generous people that like to talk and communicate. I think even with me living in the "ghetto/hood," to me, it's home. I feel it's what I'm used to and it's where I belong. Even if I was rich or had a lot of money to move somewhere nice, I think I will still consider the ghetto my home, because I think where you're raised and how you were raised depends a lot on the type of person you are and who you will grow up to be. I don't like the violence and the look of my neighborhood, but I love that it's just more than the look. It's the people. ■

ILL

IKE

NOT HAVING A FATHER, BECAUSE WHEN I MAKE IT, I CAN GIVE MY MOM ALL THE CREDIT.

A MESSAGE FUTURE – K DIFFERENC RIGHT AND

A message to my future – know the difference between right and wrong. Know your strength and weakness. Know that you are your own master. The fire of anger inside is hard to handle but not impossible. Be grateful for what you have. Don't dread over things you don't have. Stay true to yourself, respect yourself, because if you don't nobody else will. Learn from your mistakes as you go. ∎

The only thing that's impeding my success is I procrastinate a whole lot. I can't focus at all. Not even if I try to focus, I just can't focus. I also don't have motivation. I have lots and lots of ambition about what I want to do, but without the hunger and the motivation it won't ever become reality. I'm not really a hard worker. I don't really try. I think that's what is impeding my success. Also my self-esteem level is way too low. I can overcome that by working on myself. And also being hungry for what I want. ∎

TO MY [BR]OW THE [LIN]E BETWEEN WRONG.

I wish to be different at times When I stare at my life. Kids all over my community - Abuse, violence, drugs. Then me - Protected, safe, clothed, Getting by with little trouble. I wish I could help, But I'm not them, So I want to speak for them. ■

I don't think money makes a man. I don't think a man has to be straight to be a man. I don't think a man has to be all in sports to be a man. I feel being a man comes from the heart. He's a father, not a daddy. He makes mistakes. He's not perfect…nobody is. He takes care of his kids. He's there no matter what. A man is somebody that everybody looks up to, because they know, as a man, he's gonna be there. A man makes sure he has a job to take care of his family, no matter what it is. He's a father to the fatherless, biological or not. He believes in love. He believes God put love on this earth for women, men too. He has a professional, nerdy side, but then he's laid back and chilling. A man tries to do the right thing to get by. I don't think another man has to raise a man to be a man. A mother can raise him. I mean it might seem impossible, but it's not. I feel you just have to be there for him, and he will see what a man is – opposite of what the dead-beat father did. ■

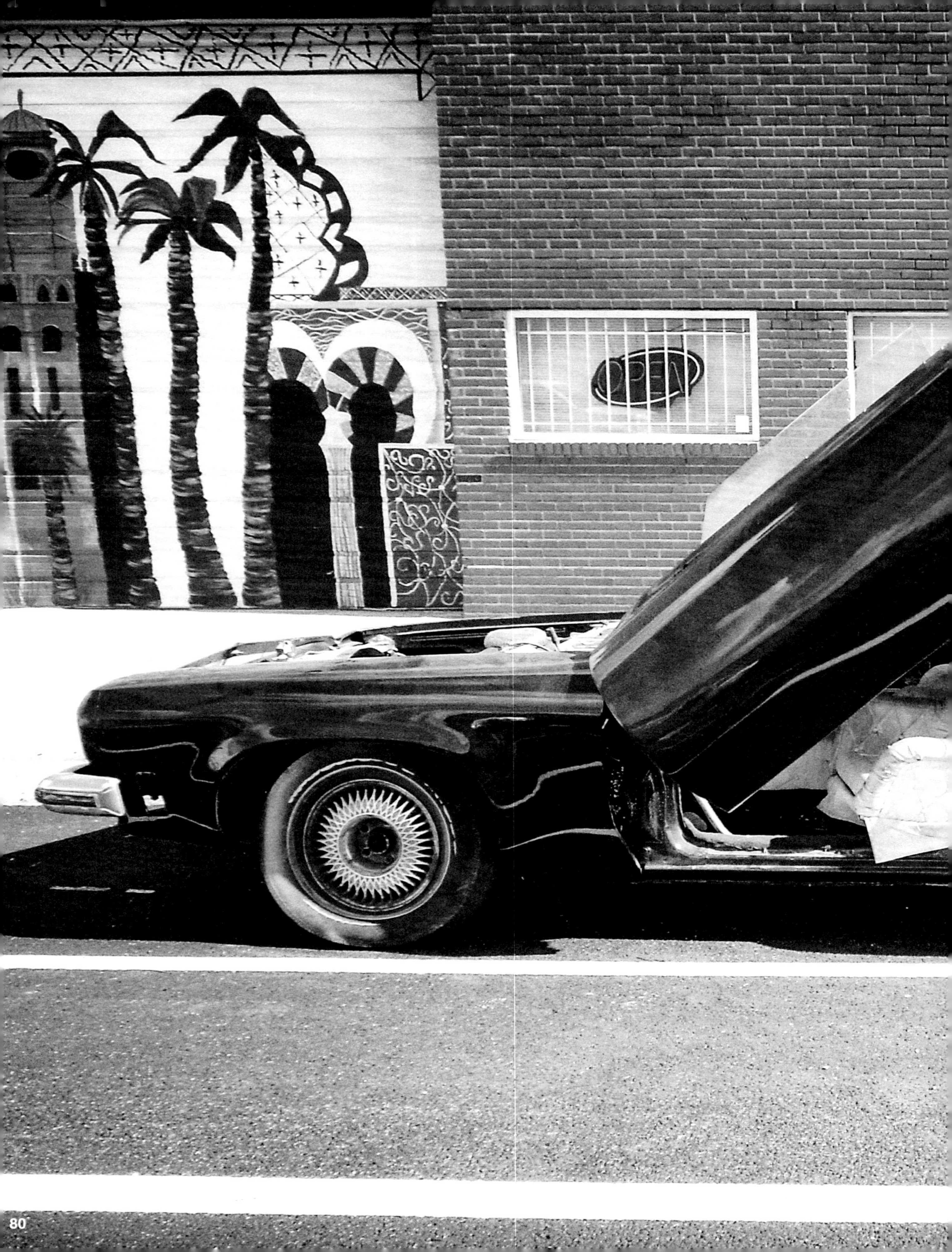
OPEN

81

People take life for granted,
Complain about things
Instead of being thankful.

Waste food,
Not thinking about how many kids starve
Everyday,
Don't have any food at all.

Brag about having new shoes, new clothes
When others
Just brag about how
They're happy to be alive. ■

Thank you God
For waking me up this morning.
First off - I'm feeling a little on edge.
Right now there is so much
That's running across my mind.

Worried, scared,
Upset, angry, disappointed.
I thought,
After my breakdown yesterday,
Everything would come together.

By 10:00pm last night
I knew nothing
Would ever be the same.

Sick to my stomach.
I wait for that call
Hoping that he's home.

Another night goes past,
And the more
He's killing himself.

I'm anxious to be
In his presence everyday.
I'm just ready to start over.

If only I could
Get him away
From the devil's circus.

Then God can be able
To restore
His heart.

In Jesus name I pray
Amen. ■

I am small,
But I stand out.
You can't get rid of me.
I'll stay forever.
You can scrub
And scrub
All you want.
I'll stay
Where I am
Just to show you that
I'll make my
Mark on this world. ■

She's weak and fragile.
They say she might die.
As tears fill my eyes,
I tell her everything
Will be alright.
As her soul prepares to go,
I close my eyes and pray.
Please God, she's so young,
Don't take my little girl away.
When I open them my heart aches
For I can sense my baby girl
Is gone. ■

   A door, it blocks my way. It stands there mocking me, laughing. I try to open it, but it won't budge. It looks so frail. But it is stronger than my will to move on. ■

   My neighborhood is an okay neighborhood. There's never people getting arrested, do to the fact that a lot of old people live there, but there is a lot of drugs and prostitution there; even though the adults think they know what's happening they really don't. They think all the drugs and prostitution happens during the night and on the streets. ■

THE DEVIL'S CIRCUS

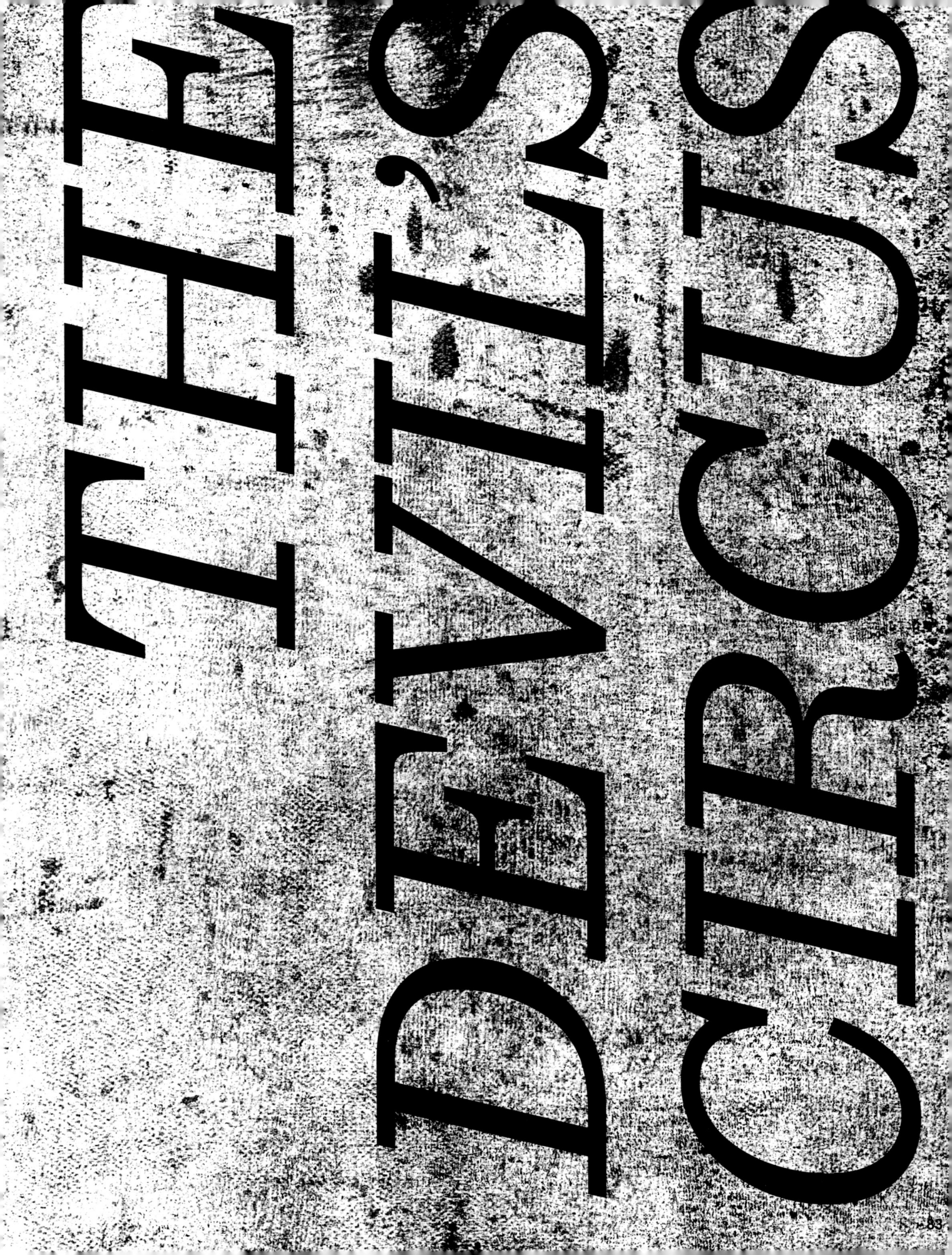

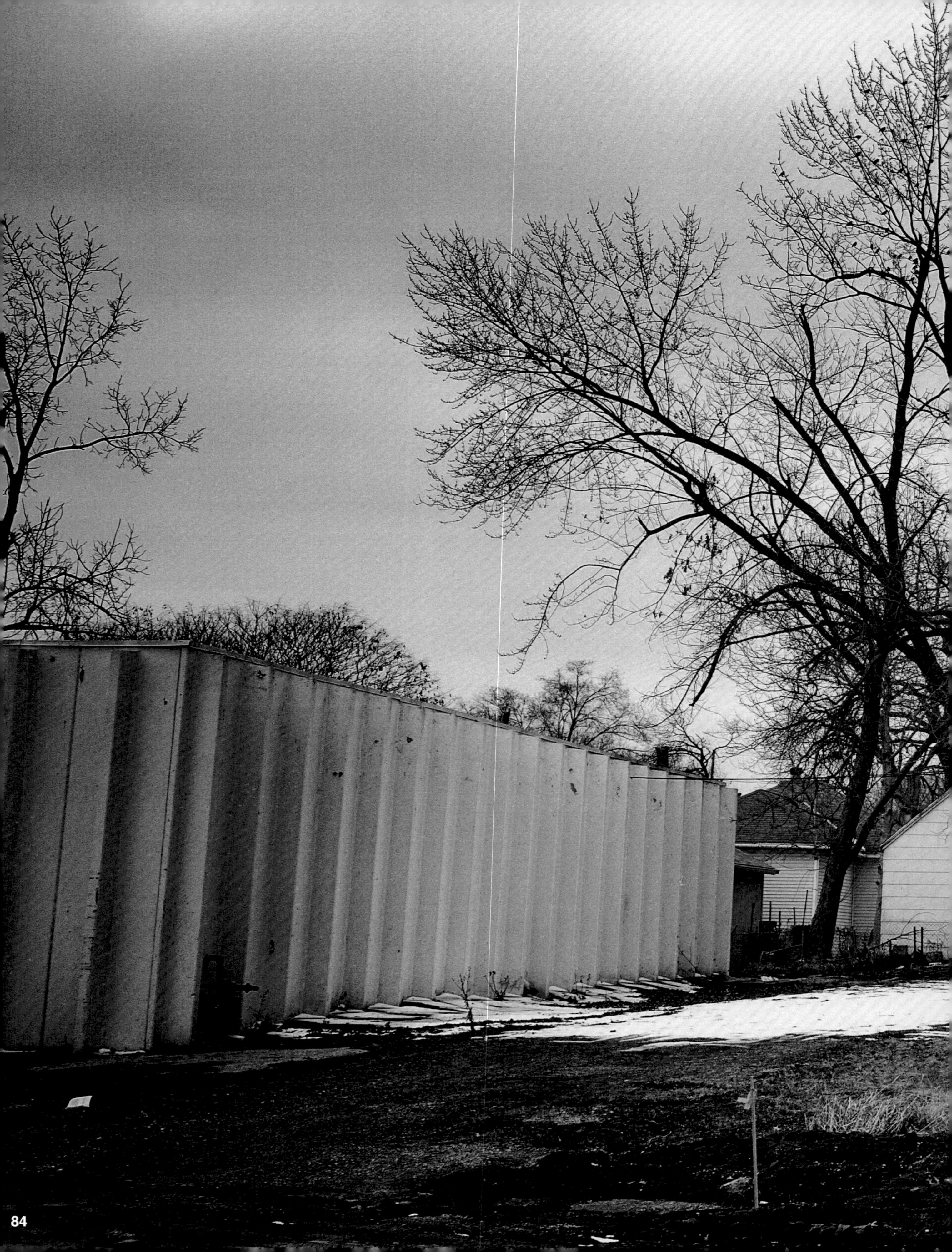

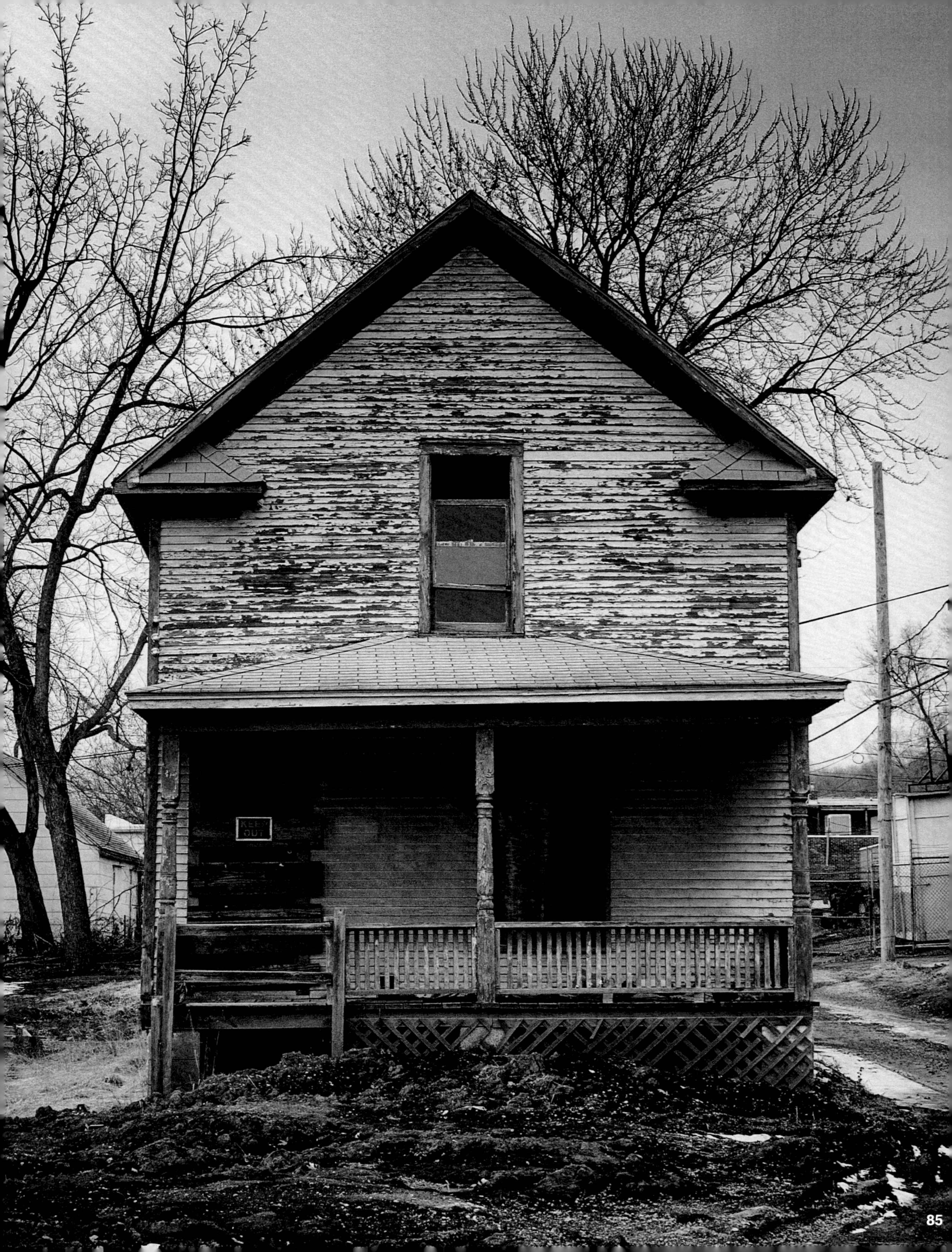
OUT

NEVER IN A MILLION YEARS WILL A MAN EVER PUT HIS HANDS ON ME.

It was a rainy and windy morning. I remember waking up sad but happy at the same time. The reason why I was sad is that I had to leave my grandpa's house, and I was happy, because I was going to see my mom. Before I left the house, I remember walking into my grandpa's room. We started talking. I wanted to go, but I didn't. I had to be strong, to not cry in front of him. "I want you to do well in school, take care, and don't worry. I'll take care of your sister," said my grandpa with a peaceful voice. I felt peace inside me. I knew my sister was going to be okay with him. My grandpa was lying down watching the news. My grandma was right beside him. I was holding my sister while sitting on the floor, and my cousin was besides us. "I don't want you to leave," said my cousin while giving me a hug. That broke my heart into pieces. I wanted to cry again, but I smiled instead of that. "But I have to," I replied, "I'll be fine. I'll be with my mom." It was time for me to leave. I hugged my sister then I told my grandpa to hold her for me. I wanted to thank my grandpa for all the things he did for me while I was living in his house. I couldn't. I didn't know how to put that in words. I couldn't express myself. So I gave him a hug and a kiss. Then I left. ■

I come from a domestic violence house. I never thought I would see half the things I seen, But I did. It taught me a lot. I will be a strong women. Not putting up with shit anyone gives me. Never in a million years Will a man ever put his hands on me.

Dear Coach/Mentor,

I appreciate you helping me improve my basketball skills and teaching me life skills that can help me all through my life. Thank you helping me even when I had an attitude or couldn't quite get some basketball skill, and you worked with me through drills and other things.

Sincerely,
Your Protégé

Everyone stood in the waiting room crying and comforting. Then I thought to myself, "Why? Why do bad things happen to good people?" At this point every memory of me and my dad raced through my head, each little thought fading away, going back into my memories, hiding like a thunderbolt hides beneath the dark clouds. We never knew why this happened. Doctors said it made no sense. He was in good health. Everything was fine. Most people can brush off a stroke and be fine. Most can do the same with a seizure too. Most people also just get a small bump when they hit their head, and most don't have that all happen in just minutes, seconds apart. My dad had no savior that hour. It wasn't till hours later when he was found and rushed to the hospital. We had two choices: keep him alive and have him live with disabilities with little to no chance of him ever recovering or just let him die. At that moment everyone was selfish. Everyone wanted to keep him. So we did. It's been four years since his accident and there is still no progress. He can't eat, sleep, walk or talk at all. He's completely paralyzed. He doesn't remember, but why does that matter when he is blind in one eye and can barely see out the other. Now we realize what should have happened. My dad was my best friend. Even though we can't laugh or play like we used to, I still put our movies on in his room and laugh how I once did, because I can see in his eyes he's laughing too somehow, and he remembers how much we loved each other and how I will always be his daughter. His disabilities changed his appearance not his heart. He will always be the loud, outrageous dad he always was. ∎

Dear Cousin,

Thanks for letting me stay over and come over whenever I want to and taking me in as a son when you don't really have to, because that's serious. Having another mouth to feed. Like I really am thankful and blessed. If I ever become rich I'll try to make sure you are successful at whatever your doing by doing whatever I can do to help. I really don't know what to say except for thank you.

Sincerely,
Me

DADs ARE SUPPOSED TO SCARE THE MONS OUT OF CLOSE

E
TERS
IY
T.

NOT BE
THEM.

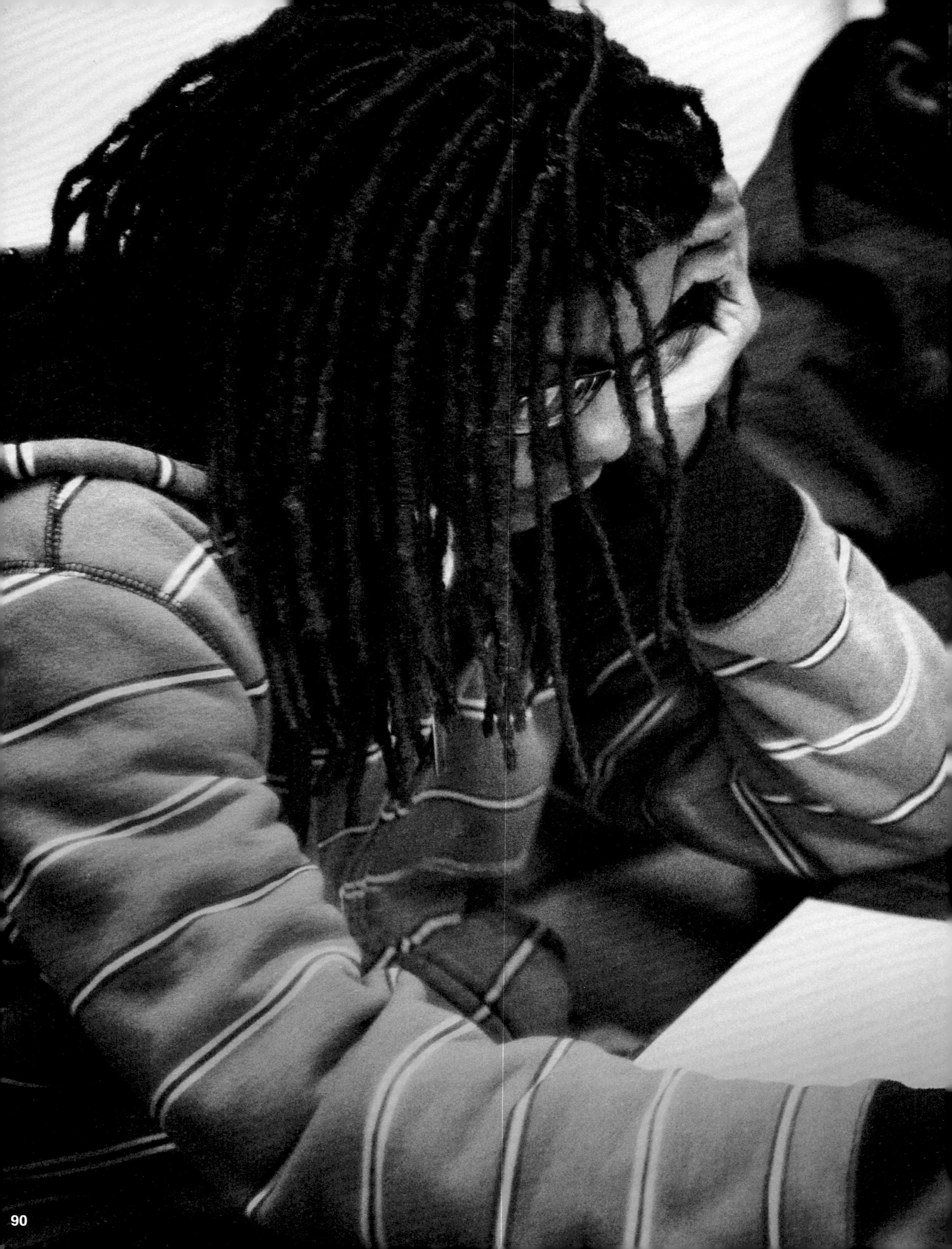

Dear Stepfather,

When I first met you I liked you. I thought you were an alright guy for my mother. I really thought that you were a good guy. Then that incident happened and my whole perspective of you changed. I was scared out of my mind, for my family, for myself. And because of that I hated you. Never in my life had I ever felt so much dislike for a person. I felt that way, because one night you got drunk and FUCKED UP. It's been 5 or 6 years since that day. I know I probably should have moved on by now but I can't forget. But I am working on being able to forgive.

Sincerely,
Your Stepdaughter

Troubles
You face in your life -
Stay away
From the violence.
I live in it.
Stay home
Rather than go places.
Fitting in isn't important.
I haven't done
Anything as a crowd
That I felt bad about.
It doesn't matter
What a group
Of kids thinks of you.
Just be you. ■

Dear Myself,

I just wanted to tell you that you are a very beautiful young lady. Don't let anyone tell you otherwise. You can be whatever you want to be. Do whatever you want to do. Don't get influenced by other people and follow behind others. Be a leader and lead by example. Don't be a follower and play catch up with others. Don't let others tell you how to live your life. It's your life. Live it how you want. Learn from your mistakes instead of reliving them. Don't worry about what somebody else has accomplished. Worry about what you want to accomplish. As long as you worry about yourself and nobody else you shouldn't have a problem. And also, I want to say I love you, and be you.

Sincerely Yours

I'm the kid with the problems.
They always ask me to be quiet.
Everyone sitting with their own kind -
I never saw anything like it.
Sometimes I'm alone,
Instantly I'm the outcast. ■

My day was going pretty good. I started my day by seeing my grandfather who I hadn't seen in almost a year. By the time we had to leave, my dad called. I answered my phone. I could tell he had been drinking. He asked where we were. My voice cracked as I said, "Grandpa's." He laughed in his drunken stooper and said, "I'm a block away at your uncle's. Come over when you leave your grandpa's." I told him that I would tell my mother. He hung up. I was a little scared. We said goodbye to my family and got in the car. As we pulled up to my uncle's house, I saw my dad leaning up against his Harley with a bottle of Jack in his hand. He started laughing. I thought to myself, oh God here we go again. I looked at my mom and said, "Please, let's just drive." She ignored me, turned off the car and got out. I watched as they fought and yelled. I laid my head into my hands. My mom got back into the car and sped off. Why does he have to do this, I thought to myself. Why would he want to start this all over again?

I started to think back to the last time this happened. I was about seven, and I remember screaming, broken glass, and seeing the flashing lights of the cop car that had pulled up. I started to shake as I remembered why they were there. They were putting my dad in handcuffs and calling him a woman beater. Then reality struck, and we pulled into the driveway.

It was pouring rain, and my mom was worried about the storm. We went into the house, and my mom turned on the news. She looked very pale with a frightened look on her face. I told her to come watch a movie with me downstairs. We were downstairs watching a movie when we heard a big crash on the hard wood floors above us. My mom and I exchanged looks. Then when we heard my dad yelling. My mom ran upstairs. I stayed in my bed, waiting, listening. It was quiet, then I heard yelling and a big bang. I ran to the top of the stairs. My heart was pounding as I yelled for my mom. No answer. All I could hear was them yelling. I ran into the living room and saw my mom and dad. I started to shake. I tried to yell stop, but nothing came out. They were in the dining room now. I blinked, and then when I opened my eyes I saw my mom falling into the kitchen. Finally I felt anger. I jumped in front of my mom and yelled, "Stay away from us." I looked at my dad and watched as the anger grew across his face. Then he was in my face yelling, screaming horrible things. I blocked him out. I thought my mom was safe behind me. He won't touch me I thought. The next thing I knew I was on the ground, and my mom was pushing my dad out the door. I got up and watched through the glass window in the door. The anger in his face had gotten worse. Finally my mom got him all the way out and locked the door. She went and sat down. I could tell she was holding back tears as she told me to go down stairs and get the phone to call 911. I was in the dining room when he threw a propane gas tank through the back window. I ran to the front room and fell to the floor, my body shaking and I could barely breathe. My mom gave me her shoes and said to get the phone from your room. She cracked on her words as she said, "Call the cops." I slipped the shoes on and walked carefully through the glass and into my room. I dialed 911, and, holding back tears, told them what happened. Five minutes later the cops and my boyfriend were there. I put my stuff in the trunk of my boyfriend's car and then got in. I watched as they cuffed my dad. He yelled, "Why Mandi? Why?" Even after all that happened I felt bad for him as we drove off. I started to cry. Then my mom took my hand and said, "You did the right thing." She pulled me close as I watched the cop lights get smaller and smaller. ∎

SHE CRACKED ON HER WORDS AS SHE SAID, "CALL THE COPS"

Just to live a lie,
So run and hope
You can escape
Your fate. ■

Words bring pain.
Let go of the past.
Who cares -
The damage is done.

Let go of the grudges.
Forgiveness.
Forgive those who hurt you.
Forgive those who doubt you.
Forgive.

Learn to love.
Forget the hatred.
You aren't getting anywhere.
Being upset is tiring.
Happiness just isn't on the menu.
But finding a way to let go
Will always be there. ■

Dear Grandma,

    I thank you for giving birth to my dad, because he taught me how to be a man even though he is in jail. Grandma you have always been there for me, taking care of me, saving me. I really thank you for that. You got me in boxing, football, basketball, swimming, karate. You made sure I was in a sport, so I won't be at home watching TV or playing the game. You taught me how to make money cutting grass, and you taught me how to ride the bus, even though you have a car. I thank you for all that you have done for me in the last 15 years. ■

Trash is all I see when I am home.
Mold is all I smell.
I hate what I have to do to them.
I can't stay here anymore.
I fight with myself to tough it out.
I find I am too weak and
Cannot overlook my sickness.
I get the courage to stand up and leave.
I cried, telling them I'm leaving.
I love them,
But I will not live like this any longer.
I tell them, "I'm sorry"
As I walk out the door.
"I will still see you," I whisper
As they wave goodbye with tears
Starting to form in their eyes.
I hold back my tears and say,
"Now my life gets better." ■

They try to break my soul.
They beat me down.
They try to make me weak.
What they don't realize is,
Every time they hit me
And try to crush me,
I grow stronger,
And they will get weaker.
For one day
Their soul,
Hope and dreams
Will disappear,
Because they thought
They could break me. ■

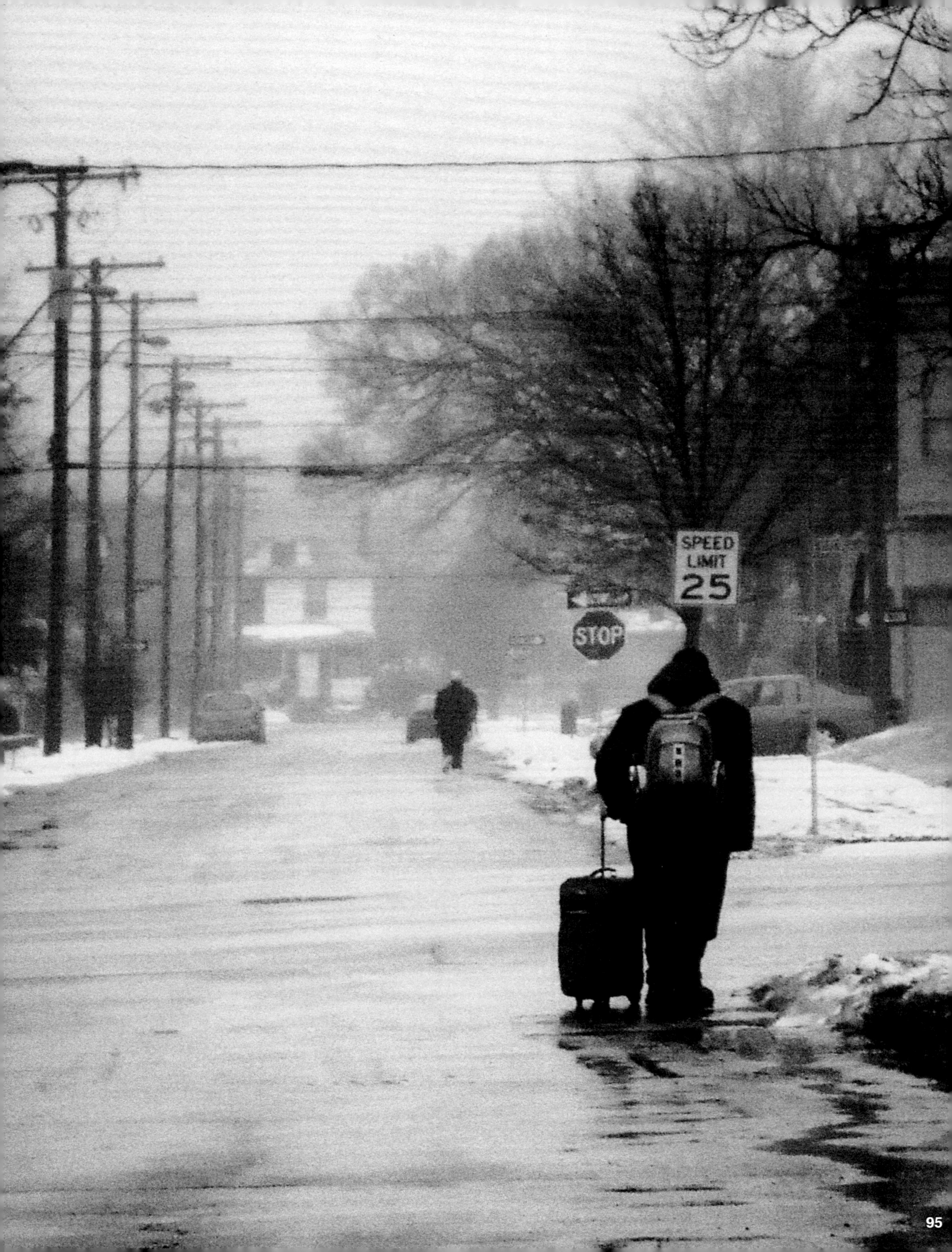
SPEED
LIMIT
25
STOP

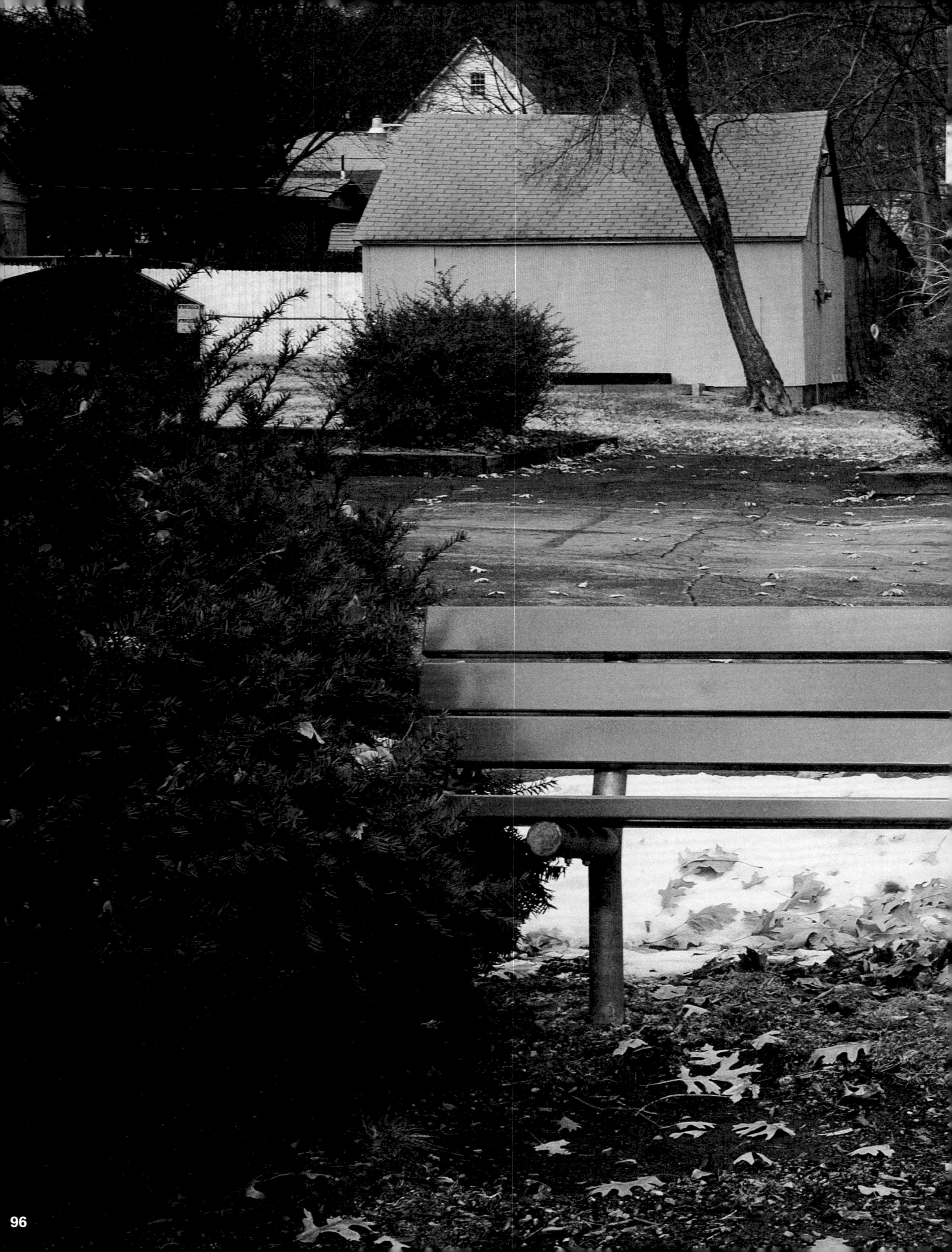

97

YOU
SOME

ARE BODY.

NOT A NOBODY.

I'M NOT YOUR
DAD, BUT I WILL
BE HERE FOR
AND YOU CAN
CALL ME DAD

I remember as a young boy I told my father, "Dad you will always be my dad. I will never call another man dad." Seeing my dad smile and saying, "I love you son", made me smile right back at him.

The first time I ever called another man "Dad" I thought about the conversation I had with my biological dad and felt guilty. Although I felt guilty, I saw that another man other than my dad loved me the same way he did. He would play catch with me, call me his son, spoil me with junk food and toys. Everything a kid could ask for my step-dad did. I knew I could call him dad, because I knew he wasn't gonna walk out of my life. I never felt a connection or trusted another man before, because I had felt abandoned by my biological dad. I felt different about my step-dad though. He changed my opinion on trust, because he actually tried to spend time with me and my family. So when I called him dad I felt guilty, but I felt relieved, because someone loved me as if I were his kid. "Dad". "Wait" I thought to myself. "I can't call him dad. Do I call him by his name instead?" I went along with it anyways. "Will you take me to the gas station?"

I remember getting in the car, and on the way there I remember thinking about how I just called another man dad. Then I thought to my self, "Maybe there isn't a problem with me calling him dad." Looking out the window I smiled to myself as we pulled into the parking lot of the gas station. Then I heard, "What do wanna get from here son?" After hearing those words some of my guilt went away, because he called me "son". Going in the store is where it all came to mind that I made the right choice, because he grabbed my hand and walked by my side as if we were father and son. After getting what I wanted, we got back in the car. That's when I asked him, "Are you my dad?" He looked at me, then looked at the road and thought about his answer. He looked at me again and said, "I'm not your dad, but I am your step-dad." I got a little depressed, because I didn't know what a "step-dad" was, then he explained. "I'm not your dad, but I will be here for you, and you can call me dad." Walking back up the stairs to the house, I remember telling him, "I'm glad you're my dad." He replied, "Me too son, me too." Our relationship has grown over the years as the relationship with my biological dad disintegrated. I couldn't ask for a better dad. ■

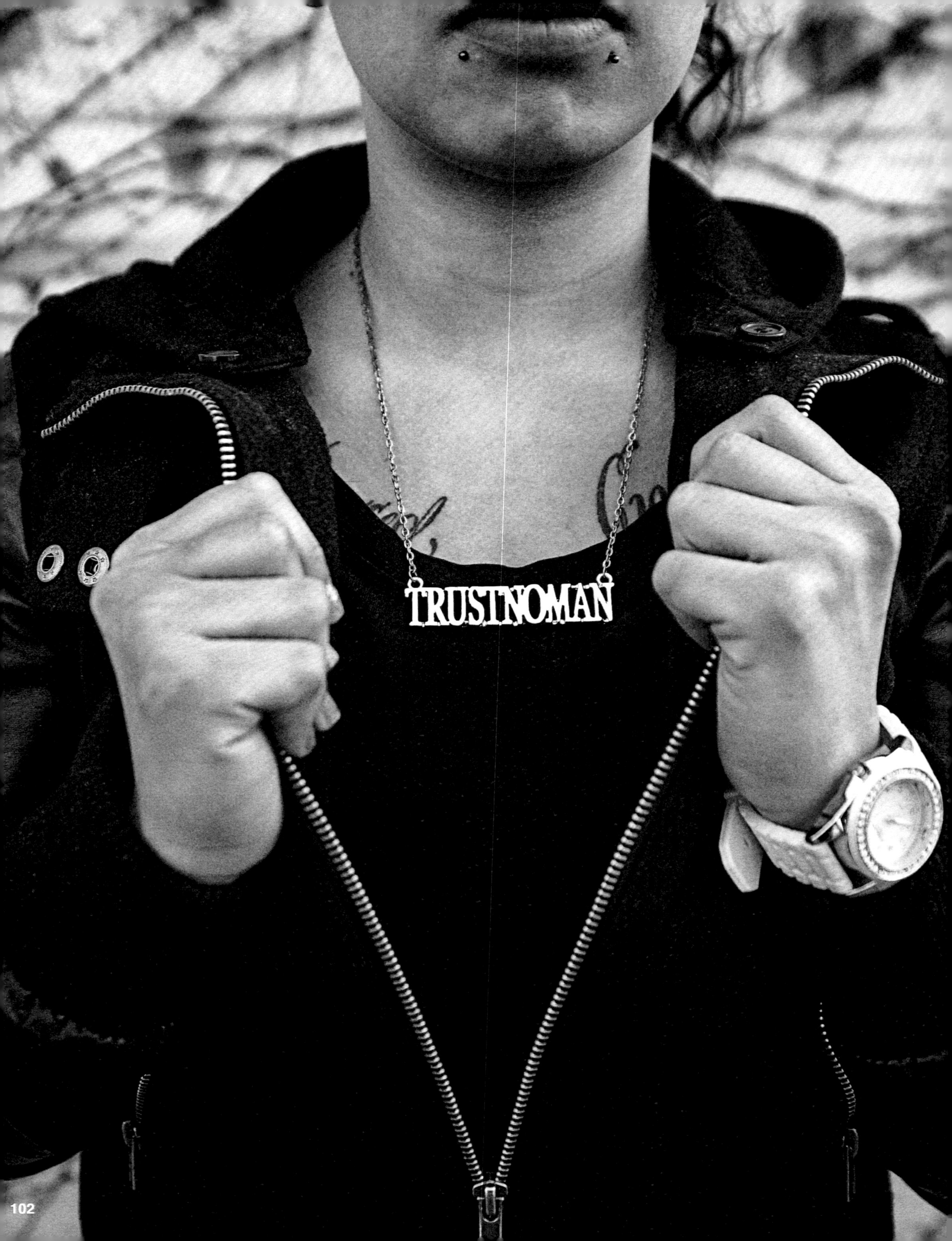
TRUSTNOMAN

STRANGE GIRL – HER FATHER'S BRUTALITY ONLY MAKES HER STRONGER

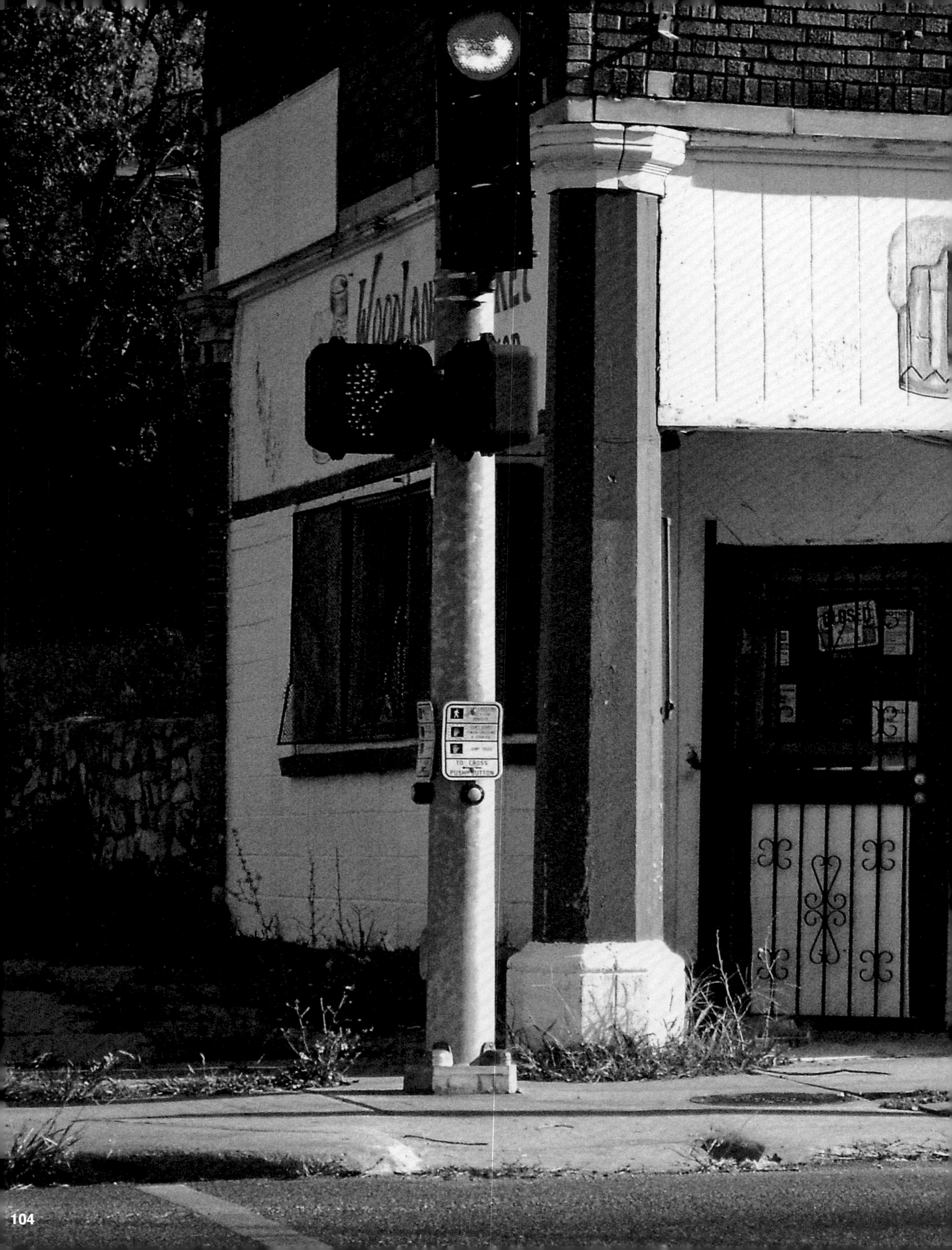
CLOSED
TO CROSS
PUSH BUTTON

WOODLAND MARKE
GROCERIES & LIQUOR
ATM
MACHINE
Available
Inside
Coldest Beer in

I AM SORRY WALLS. YOU HAVE SEEN AND FELT SO MANY THINGS.

Being at home is hard.
I don't want to be here.
The walls are filled with bad memories.
It's hard to fake a smile,
When all I want to do is cry.
Sitting here, thinking about everything
These walls have seen and heard.
It scares me to think of the fights.
I am sorry walls.
You have seen and felt so many things.
People have hit you,
Made holes in you, and
I feel bad for you.
These walls – they have seen things
And heard things
They should not have.
You have heard everything
That has hurt me.
You have felt my pain
And I have felt yours. ■

This is about finding a way to let go.
A way to let go
Of what you've lost.
A way to let go
Of bottled up feelings.

Finding a way
Of freeing yourself
Of what bogs you down.

Letting go,
To reach for new heights. ■

I think people change in some way, not in all ways. Like my mom's friend - she come over to my house, and almost every day she do crack and wet. Like one day she over my house, and we all was inside, and she called some man over to my mom's house. She was smoking wet on the pourch, and I came outside and was like that smell, and she didn't say anything. She was looking at me like she was dead. I called my mama outside, and I was like mama what that smell, and she was like hold on, and she call her friend outside, and she was like you was smoking that shit on my pourch, and I was like what wet? My mama told her to leave her house, and get her shit and leave. They was cussing each other out and stuff. She said you don't ever need to come back to my f***ing house no more with that shit. One day she came over and look deffernt, and she just got even mess up, cus she got on that stuff more, and then she went to this place and got better. She living a better life than she was. ■

A girl hides
While her father yells.
She wonders why
Her mother hasn't left him yet.
Maybe she's scared for her life.
The girl is strong.
She has courage.
She is determined
To not let the cycle
Continue.
Strange girl –
Her father's brutality
Only makes her stronger. ■

Dear Little Brother,

I'm sorry I don't stay with you and mom anymore. You're too young to understand what's going on between our family, which would explain why we don't go see great grandma, even though she is very sick with cancer. I know you want me to stay every night in your little cars bed, rocking you to sleep like I did when you were just born and Mom left without saying a word to gamble our money away. You are getting so big, so strong, so brave. You are becoming a man, because it's just you and Mom. You try to do so much, even though you're so young, but you can't do everything alone and do it without thinking first. I will always be waiting for you with open arms and a place to stay.

Love,
Your Big Sister

I know.
I know how it feels not to be accepted.
I was rejected and
Straight out disowned.
I realize now
I can finally be happy
When I accept myself.
I was fat.
I got called names that had me
Wanting to kick ass.
Depression took it toll.
I cut. I cut. I abused myself.
When I looked in the mirror
All I saw were the words I was called.
I've risen, and I've fallen.
I have been knocked down.
I'm scared to get up.
I know.
I know.
I know what it feels to be
Controlled by your emotions.
Life's a bitch, and
I'm its puppet. ■

IT ONLY T[AKES]
ONE SMA[LL]
DECISIO[N TO]
CHANGE [THE]
WHOLE [...]

AKES
LL
TO
YOUR
IFE.

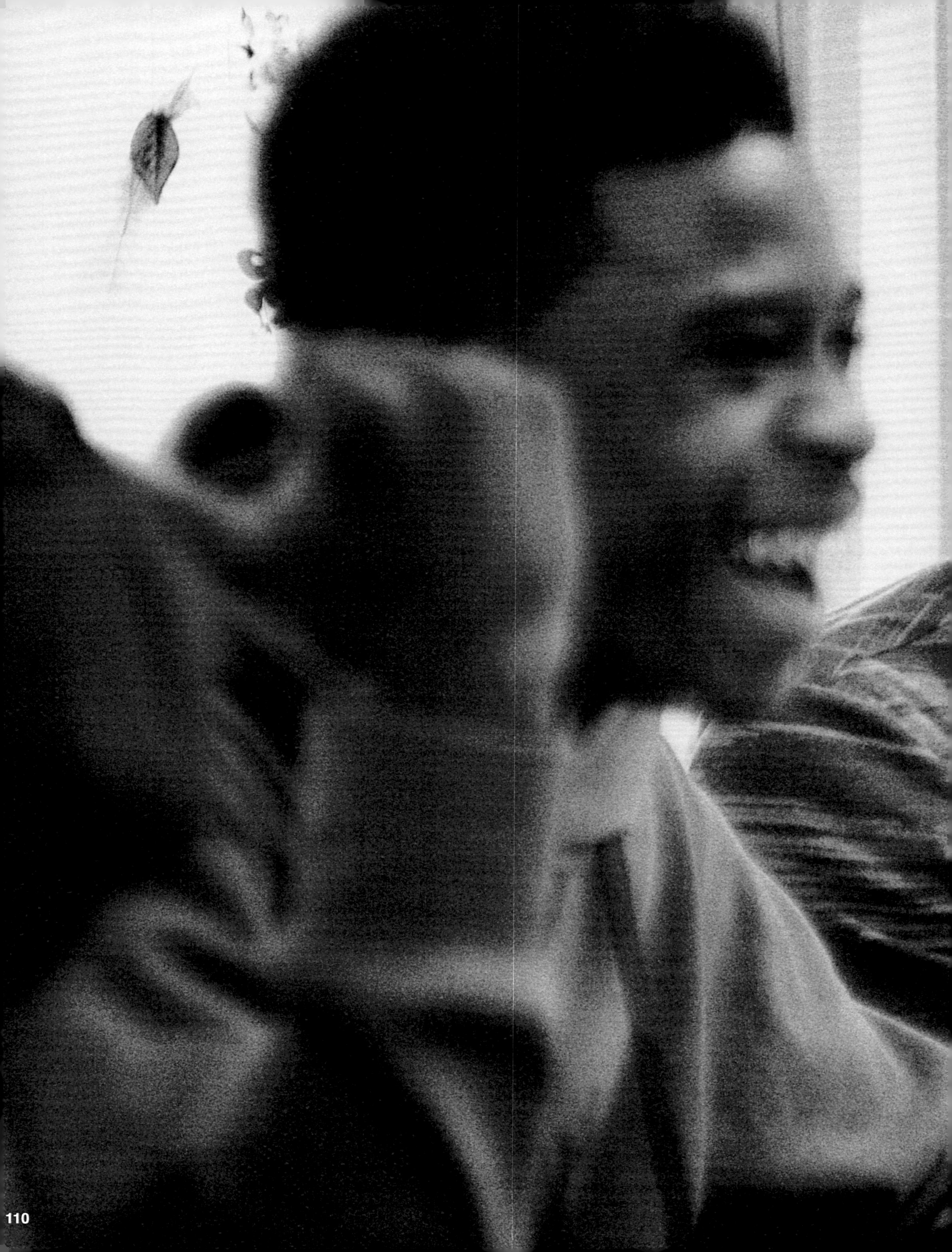

111

I WOULD NEVER WANT MY KID TO EVER HAVE TO SEE HOW BAD THE WORLD IS.

Mommie -
What do I have to do for you to see me?
Do I have to stand on an abandoned stage
doing a hiccup dance day in and day out?

Mommie -
I always feel like we are two different planets
who crossed paths by complete accident
but got stuck with each other anyway.
Me, a brazen, unkempt, and sometimes snotty little girl,
and you, just like the Red Sea -
always parting your legs for a man posing as God
but never seeing the holiness in your daughter's eyes.

It all started with a little curiosity, starting to like boys and trying to see what they actually wanted from me. By the time I was 14, I started drinking and having sex. One day I discovered I was pregnant. So young and scared to tell anybody, I waited for 6 months just hoping this would go away. But I just got bigger and bigger. Then and there I was losing my childhood. It was guaranteed that I could no longer do what I wanted, when I wanted to. It's like being held prisoner of my own life. So months passed by, and I finally had a little boy. I have to admit I was so angry with him, because he was the reason I couldn't go have fun anymore. But then I realized it was me. I'm responsible, and it was now my job to keep his childhood alive. ∎

Being a man is being able to take care of yourself or take care of your family in your environment. If you live in the ghetto then you might have to be tough, but if you live in the suburbs you can be a little softer. But all men should take responsibility. To raise a man just read the bible, and it will have all of the instructions that you need. Also you have to know how to fight and when to fight, because you can't go around getting beat up. But you should still know how to solve a problem without using violence. ∎

If I could give you advice -
Honestly, what can this 14 year old tell you? But I can tell you to keep ya head up. You are somebody, Not a nobody. Don't feel inadequate. You are better that that 10 letter word. Be you, and take no BS. ∎

My brother from Texas went and robbed some people on the Plaza. I saw him do it. He went to jail and got out. I was at home, and I was bored, so I pulled out my Dad's gun, and I said to myself, "Let's go rob somebody." Then I said, "No," and I put the gun back where it was from. ∎

It only takes one small decision
To change your whole life.
The drugs…the gangs…
Juvenile Hall…
It only takes on small decision
To change your whole life.
Why did I think
That those things were all
That ever mattered in my life?
It only takes one small decision
To change your whole life.

Was it the people I hung out with?
Was it that I was young and stupid?
Or was it all a part of a life plan?
It only takes one small decision
To change your whole life.

Maybe it was those reasons
I made the decisions I made.
But now that's over,
And my life from now on
Will be trouble sober. ■

Pisses me off
Quiet and shy
Can't be outgoing
And loud.
Quiet and alone at parties.
Why?
I choose to be.
Can't speak loud enough
At restaurants
Or somewhere public.
Always left out
Of the group.
Trying to get better.
Trying to get out
Of my comfort zone.
I won't give up.
I want to be
Part of the group.
I want to be heard. ■

Myself -
No one can stand in my way.
Nothing can stand in my way.
The only way I will stop
Is if I stop myself -
Only if I get in my own way. ■

Dear Teacher,

    Thank you for everything you have done for me. It really means the world to me. You pushed me to do more challenging things and stay in your honors class rather than dropping out of it. You helped me afterschool with work I didn't understand. You listened to me when I had problems going on in my life, and you let me know it was going to be okay. You kept telling me to go to AP classes this year, and I am very sorry that I am not going to do it. You made a wonderful impact on my life. I know now I can do anything I set my mind to, because you told us we could. You never let your classes down. You pushed us to do more in life and helped us try to meet our goals. I just want to say, "Thank you so much for everything you have done. You truly are the best teacher ever!" ■

Student

Sitting there, hoping they're okay.
Knowing who made those bullets pop.
Hearing those 10 rounds blasted.
Sirens coming from every direction.
Listening to the news, "Four teens shot
Outside the local community center."
So angry, because I knew
It was going to happen.
Worried about them,
Wondering if they were alive.
Nothing has changed.
Can't open their eyes.
It's only a matter of time
Before another bullet targets
them again. ■

Dear Momma,

I miss and hope you are okay. I was so mad when I seen you in that car, but you never had the time to tell the person that was driving to stop, so you could see your son. And I was so hurt, because it looked like you were on drugs. I walked home mad and disappointed, because you said you were done with drugs. Why don't you try to come see me or call? I feel like you don't love me no more and wanted to know who's my real father. You told Nana, but you can't tell that hurts me. But it's okay, I'll find him one of these day. Until then, focusing on my education and playing ball, and hope I make it to the NBA, because I want to buy you a house, car, and anything you need. But I just need for you to get better, so I can do this all of this. I don't want to see you waste your life on drugs. But Nana has been taking care of me, and it's been great living with her. I'm just writing, because I love you. ■

"When I was 5 or 6 I was up in my mom's room watching TV. I thought the people in the TV looked hungry, so I put my peanut butter and jelly in the DVD player and then I had some milk and I put it in the back of the TV cause I thought the people needed something to drink. ■

The future,
Not set in stone.
I can change it,
Change my mind,
Change the future.
Anything can happen.
It's my future.
I can change it. ■

Hello, do you remember me?
I am that little flower
That you picked at petal by petal.
All you left me with was a stem
With no more pretty petals to be looked at.
You thought it would make me ugly and unnoticeable,
But you forgot to pull me up from my roots.
And one day, I was noticed,
And I was watered and nourished
With unconditional love.
Now look at me.
I am growing again
With pretty petals that can be noticed
From a mile away.
Just so you know,
You didn't break me.
You actually helped me become
The beautiful flower I am today. ■

I don't feel nothing is keeping me from success. I feel that if you wanna be successful, nothing is holding you back from that. I don't care where you're from or who you are. You can be successful. I have heard so many say they want to make it out of the ghetto, but they're stuck. That's not true. I feel jobs need people like us that live in bad neighborhoods that went through some things, because we would know what it feels like, and we are more helpful in certain situations. Anybody can do anything as long as you work hard, trust in God and get an education. I feel that we could be the best at our jobs, because something in the ghetto inspires us to want to do better and have a better life for ourselves and our families. I don't think nothing is holding me back, you back, the yellow man back, or the purple woman back, because we can do ANYTHING. ■

The earliest childhood memory that I have is when I was 4 and my mom left me and my younger brother at home by ourselves. We, as kids, really didn't look at anything as a threat or danger. So, she left us at night and my dad came over and knocked on the door. We didn't answer the door at first cause my mom said not to. So for a long time we didn't. My dad was persistent. We ended up opening up the door. When we opened up the door, my dad gathered all of our things and took us with him. Ever since then, we never really got a chance to spend time with my mom. Now, my mom is in prison facing time over a murder charge. So, if you think you can help me overcome a fear like that, I would be happy to know it." ■

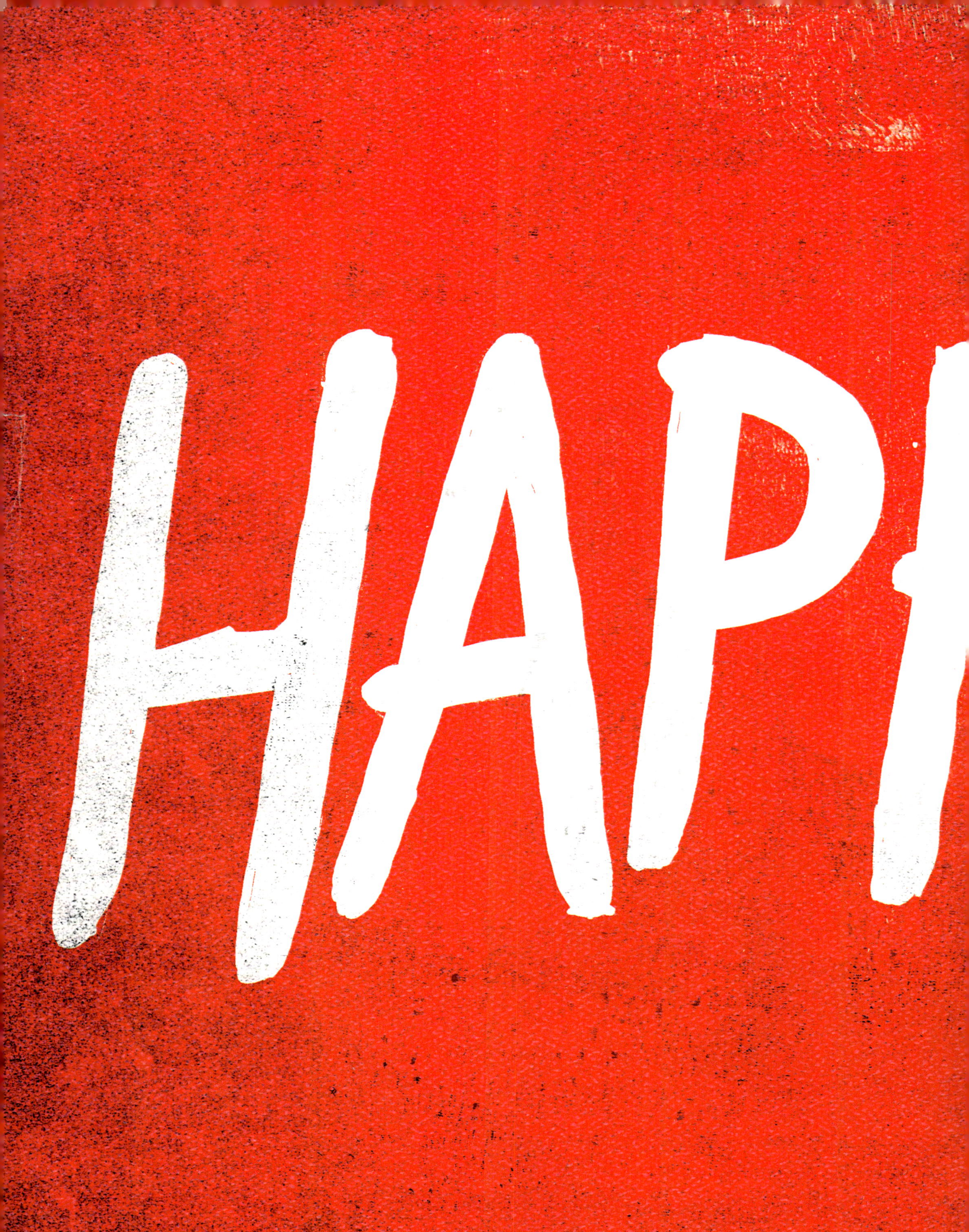
HAP

OY TO BE ALIVE.

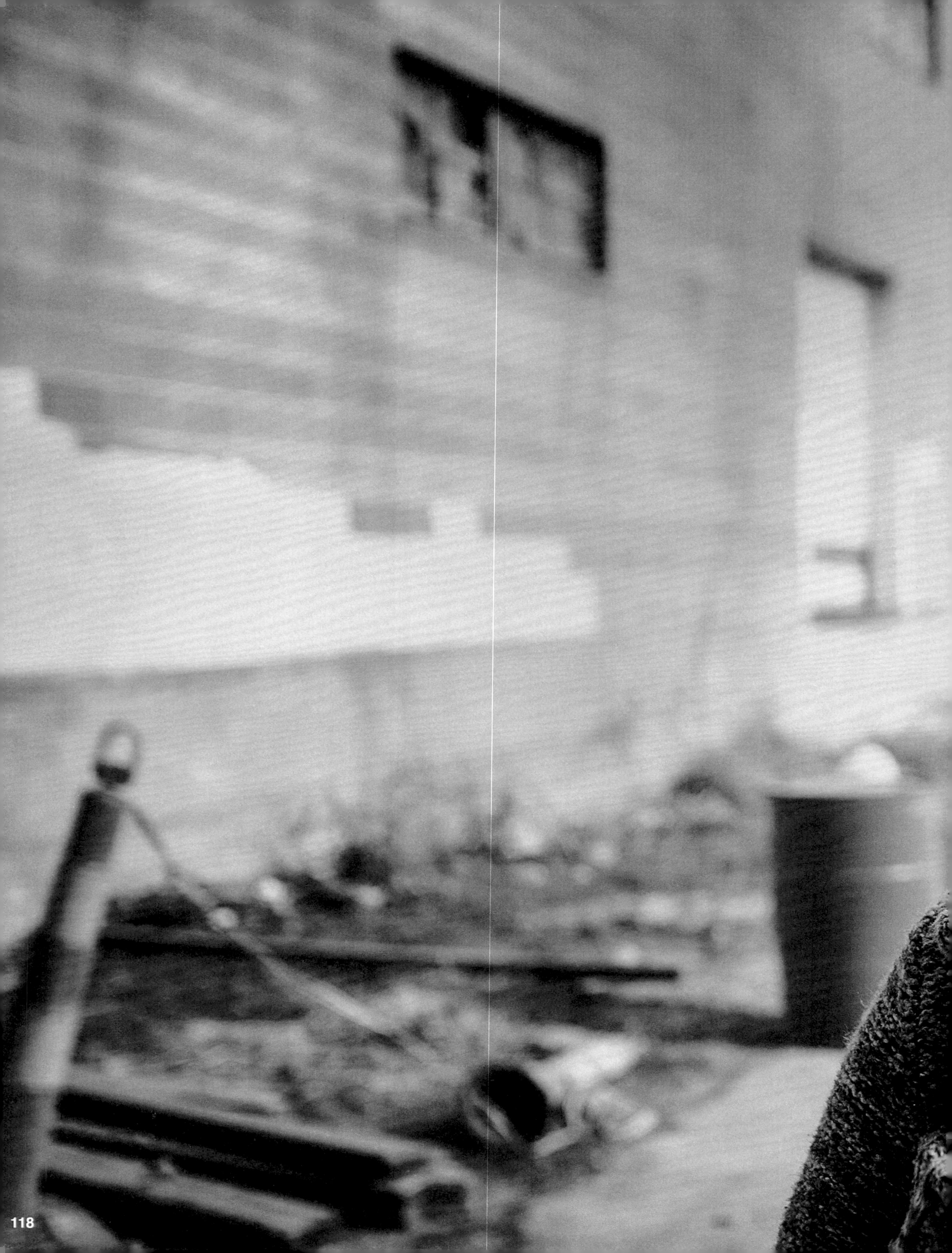

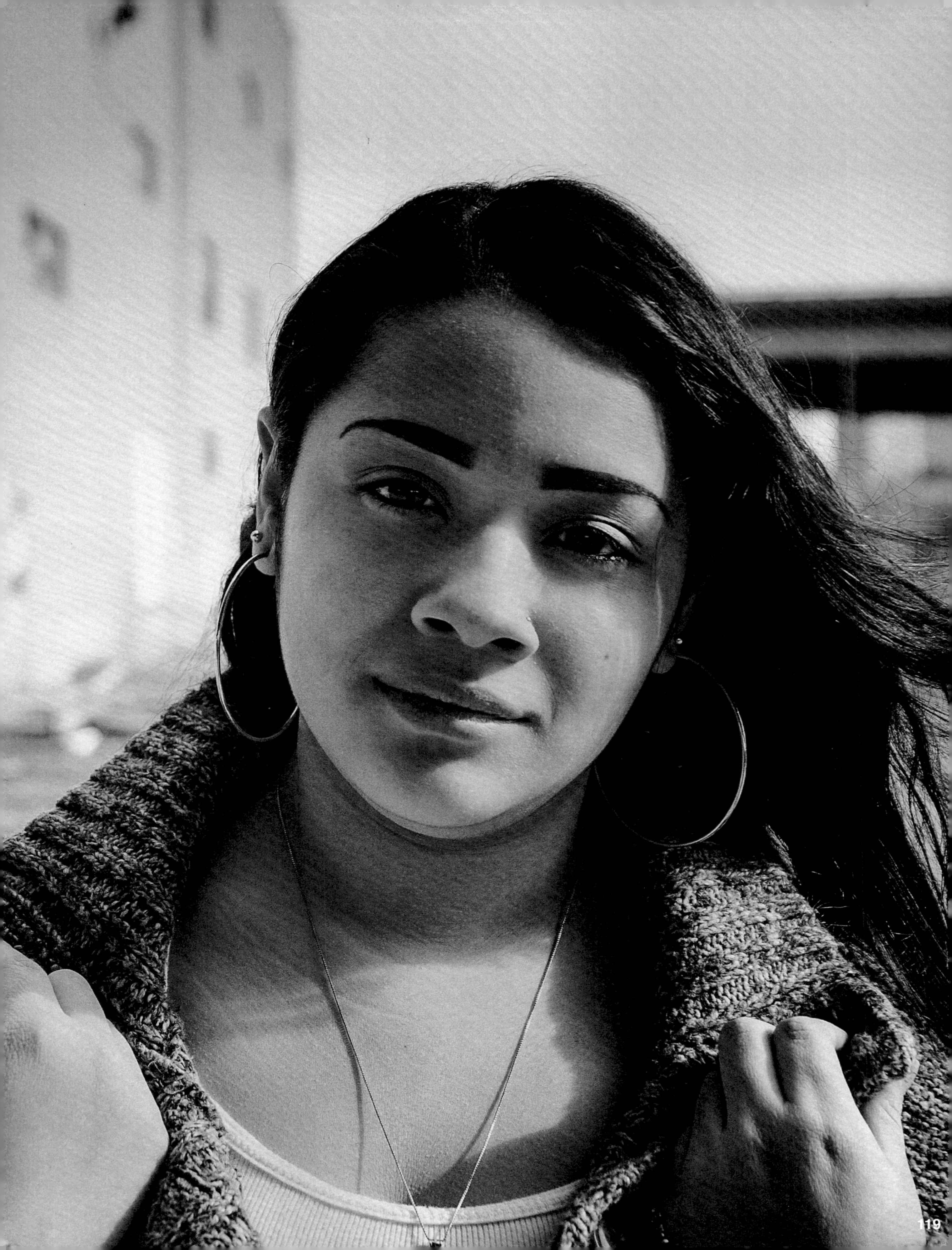

*IT'S MY FUTURE.
I CAN CHANGE IT.*

How the Eagle & the Elephant Became Friends

Janice Santikarn
Illustrated by Prateep Paisarnnan

Printed exclusively for
Royal Thai Embassy,
Washington, DC, U.S.A.

In commemoration of the 180th Anniversary
of Thai-US Relations, 1833-2013.

First printed in Thailand by Sirivatana Interprint, 2012

© 2012 Royal Thai Embassy, 1024 Wisconsin Avenue NW, Suite 401
Washington, DC 20007, U.S.A.

All rights reserved. No part of this book may be reproduced, stored in a retrieval system or transmitted in any form or by any means, electronic, mechanical, photocopying, and recording or any other information storage and referral system without the prior written permission of the copyright owner.

ISBN 978-616-305-293-3

Sirivatana Interprint Public Company Limited
Bangkok, Thailand

"C'mon Ben, finish your breakfast. I need to leave early this morning."
"What's the rush, dad?"
"I have a meeting at the State Department. Mr. Davis asked to see me."
"Uh oh, hauled in by the boss, huh? Hope you don't get detention!"
"Ha, ha. That's very funny.
OK, wise guy, grab your bag. I'll drop you at school on my way."

"Good morning, sir."
"Hi Tom, thanks for coming in.
Please, sit down. Let me get right to the point. It seems our new President is very impressed with your work; so impressed that he would like to offer you a promotion. How does the position of U.S. Ambassador…"

"Wow!" At the mention of the word 'Ambassador', Tom stopped listening and his mind began swirling with images … where would he be located?

"...to Thailand, sound?" the chief was asking. "It's a long way from the United States of America, but our two countries have had a close relationship for a long time, dating all the way back to 1833 when the USA and Thailand signed the Treaty of Amity and Commerce. That makes Thailand the oldest non-European ally the U.S. has."

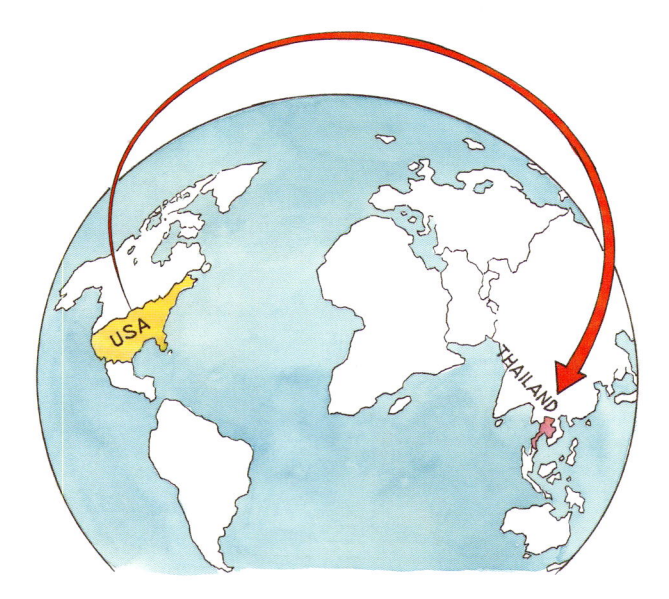

"Anyway," Mr. Davis continued, "you'll find much more information in the file we have prepared. Good luck, Tom! I'm sure you'll do a great job!"

At dinner that night Tom Roberts looked across the table at his son Ben and his wife Carol and coughed to get their attention. "Ahem! I have some important news to share. Guess what? I have just been appointed U.S. Ambassador to Thailand," he announced, grinning proudly. Ben's eyes widened. "Wow, cool, dad, congratulations! But wait a minute, where exactly is Thailand... and when are we going ...and what can I take with me?"
Mr. Roberts held up his hand. "Whoa, Ben," he chuckled. "Finish your dinner first. I'll answer all your questions later."

After dinner, Ben's father pointed to a map on the computer screen. "Thailand is in Southeast Asia. It is the only Southeast Asian country never to have been colonized by a European power and has always been independent. Some people say the country is shaped like an axe or perhaps an elephant's head and trunk. You can see that it shares borders with Laos to the north, Cambodia to the east, Myanmar to the west and Malaysia in the south."

"Thailand and the USA have been friends for almost 200 years. Back then, it was called Siam – you've probably heard of Siamese cats and Siamese twins - but Siam was the name foreigners gave to the country. The Thai people call it Thailand, which means 'the land of the free', and since 1939 it has been known as the Kingdom of Thailand. Do you have any questions?"

Before Ben could answer, his mom spoke up. "What about Ben? Are there good schools in Thailand?" "Sure," said Ben's dad. They have great schools. However most of them teach in the Thai language, which is rather complicated for non-Thai speakers to pick up quickly. English has only one tone and 26 letters, whereas Thai has five tones and 44 letters, plus another 32 vowels! But don't worry, there are also several very good international schools that teach in English – and some of those follow the American education system. So he'll be fine."

Just then Ben cut in. "Dad, I just remembered! What about Sammy, our pet eagle, can he come with us?" "Don't worry, I've already spoken to Mr. Davis about that," his father said. He told me that the economic, trade and friendship treaties between the USA and Thailand have often been called the Eagle-Elephant agreements, so he thinks Sammy would be a great symbol of the relationship between our two countries. As long as we get the proper paperwork done there shouldn't be a problem."

As the plane descended, Ben Roberts peered out the window for his first look at Bangkok. He had learned from a magazine on board that the Thai people gave the city another name*, which was actually the longest name of any capital city in the world. However, this was much too long to use every day so most Thais just shortened it to 'Krung Thep', which meant the 'City of Angels'.

Ben knew that Thailand was divided into four regions, with Bangkok located in the Central and Eastern section. Through this area ran the Chao Phraya River, which he could now clearly see snaking its way through the huge sprawling city below. There were about 68 million people in Thailand and around 10 - 12 million lived in Bangkok. Leaning closer, Ben noted several clusters of modern office towers and high-rise apartments in the city center gradually giving way to thousands of smaller houses on the outskirts. Beyond that, were acres and acres of green fields where farmers grew rice and cultivated crops in the fertile flatlands around the river.

Once they cleared customs, Ambassador Roberts, his wife, and Ben were quickly whisked away to their new home located in the city center.

*Krung Thep Mahanakhon Amon Rattanakosin Mahinthara Ayuthaya Mahadilok Phop Noppharat Ratchathani Burirom Udomratchaniwet Mahasathan Amon Piman Awatan Sathit Sakkathattiya Witsanukam Prasit

The rest of the weekend Ben mostly slept, jetlagged after the 24 – hour trip from Washington, D.C. to Bangkok. However, by late Monday morning he managed to drag himself downstairs in time to hear his parents discussing the day's plans.

"I need to be at the Palace by 11 a.m.," his dad was saying.

Ben was suddenly wide-awake.

"Whoa, dad, the Palace?"

"Well, Ben, my job as Ambassador means that here in Thailand I represent the President of the United States. So the first thing I need to do is meet with the Thai Head of State and present my credentials to him."

"But that's the Prime Minister, right? Why do you need to go to the Palace?"

"Actually, no. Back home the President is the Head of Government as well as the Head of State, but here in Thailand the roles are divided. Since 1932 Thailand has had a constitutional monarchy, which means that the King of Thailand is the Head of State while the Prime Minister, appointed from among Members of Parliament chosen at the general election, is the Head of Government."

Ambassador Roberts looked at his watch. "Hmm, I need to get moving. What are your plans today, Ben? School doesn't start for a few days yet."

"Oh, I might just hang out here...maybe take a swim later."

Up in his room, Ben chatted online with some friends back home, but although it was only 11 a.m. in Bangkok it was 11 p.m. in D.C., and on a Sunday night most of his friends were already asleep. After the earlier conversation with his father, Ben was curious about the Thai King, so now he decided to search the 'net' for more information.

The first thing he learned surprised him. King Bhumibol Adulyadej wasn't born in Thailand. He was actually born in the USA on the 5th of December 1927 in Cambridge, Massachusetts... and he had reigned since 1946! "Wheeeww", whistled Ben, "that's a whole lot longer than the four-year terms of American Presidents! The people must like him a lot." As he read more, Ben realized this was true. The King really was greatly loved by his people, for right from day one he had worked hard to improve their wellbeing and develop the nation.

Before he shut down his laptop, one more item caught Ben's eye; pictures of the King playing saxophone with the great American jazz musicians Benny Goodman, Stan Getz and Lionel Hampton. Apparently the King of Thailand not only played saxophone, but also piano, trumpet and cornet. What's more, he composed jazz music, painted, and was an author and photographer too. "Wow!"

Grabbing a towel, Ben headed outdoors in search of the pool. It was not even lunchtime yet and the temperature had already hit the 90's. Following a path toward the rear of the large compound, he came upon a small wooden house with its window shutters propped open to let in the breeze.

Peering inside, he was surprised by the face of a Thai boy who suddenly popped up in front of him.
"Who are you?" the stranger asked.
"Er, who are you?"
"I asked first!"
"I'm Ben, I've just moved in."
"Oh, you must be the new Ambassador's son. I'm Jai. My dad's the gardener. What are you doing?"
"I was looking for the pool, but I guess I took the wrong path."
"Wait there," said Jai. "I'll show you where it is."

The pool was on the other side of the grounds and as the boys passed by the main house, Jai stopped and pointed to a birdcage on the verandah.

"Wow! What is that? I've never seen a bird like that before." Ben brought Jai closer. "This is Sammy. See, his name is on the metal tag attached to his leg. He is an American Bald Eagle, the National Emblem of the USA. Not so long ago it was an endangered species, but thanks to breeding programs the numbers are much greater nowadays. Even so, we still had to get special permission to bring him with us."

From there, Jai pointed Ben in the direction of the pool.
"Follow that path and you can't miss it. Listen, tomorrow's my little sister's birthday. Would you like to come by our house in the morning and join in the celebrations?"
"Thanks, that would be great. I'll see you then," said Ben.

The next morning Ben returned to the small house at the foot of the garden. Upon meeting Jai's mother and father, he made sure to 'wai' them, putting his hands together and bringing them up to his chin. His mom had told him how important this was and made sure he knew how to do it properly. For Thais, it was not only like shaking hands, it was also a way to show respect, by bowing the head lower when greeting people of older age or of a higher position.

"You're just in time," said Jai. We're about to start. My sister Joop is going to release some birds. Like most Thais, we are Buddhists, and we believe that if you do good things in your life, you will receive good things in return - it's called 'making merit'. So on special occasions like this, we do a good deed like releasing trapped birds or fish."

"Now, come and meet my sister.
Joop, where are you? The birds are here.
Jooooop! Joooop! Hmmm, where is she?"
At last a small Thai girl came running toward them from the Ambassador's house.
"Where've you been?" asked Jai.
"We're waiting for you to open the cages."
Jai's little sister looked confused.
"Open the cages? What do you mean?
I've already released the bird."
Now it was Jai who looked confused.
"But the birds are still here."
"No, not those," Joop explained.
"The strange looking bird over there. I set it free."

Ben and Jai looked at each other in horror before racing toward Sammy's cage. But it was too late. The door was open and he was gone. Frantically they began to search. Jai scoured the nearby bushes and trees calling Sammy's name, while Ben looked up into the bright light, scanning the blue skies.

Precious seconds ticked by before Ben suddenly pointed upward.
"There he is! I can see the sunlight reflecting off his nametag."
He called out. "Sammy, Sammy, come down!" But the eagle didn't obey. He continued flying in slow wide circles until one powerful flap of his wings sent him soaring over the fence.

Rushing to the front gate, the boys yanked it open and were met by a blaring mass of cars, trucks, buses and motorbikes. To the left and right, sidewalks bustled with office workers, tourists and vendors, while above them smoke from chicken pieces roasting on coal-fired grills rose into the air. Peering through the spiraling gray plumes, Ben and Jai once again spotted the flash of light.

"He's getting away," yelled Jai. "Quick, come with me." Following him to the roadside, Ben watched as the Thai boy held out an arm, gently waved his hand up and down and stopped an approaching vehicle. After exchanging a few words with the driver, Jai turned to Ben. "C'mon, jump in." As the little 3-wheeled vehicle sped away from the curb, Ben looked puzzled. "Don't worry," said Jai. "It may not look like it, but this is a taxi – we call it a 'tuk-tuk'. I asked the driver to follow the bird. Let's keep an eye out for Sammy and point the way."

The eagle took them on a meandering tour of the city before finally leading them to the river. The Chao Phraya played an important part in the lives of the Thai people. Most of the population was engaged in agriculture and industry, and the river and its waterways were used to ship products such as rice and teak wood from upcountry down to Bangkok for export. In addition, the river's smaller system of canals, or 'klongs', were vital for transportation, washing and fishing, as well as playing a large role in the drainage of floodwaters out to sea during the rainy season.

Without warning, the eagle suddenly swooped down to settle amongst the pointed golden pagodas of a nearby complex. Following closely, the boys leapt from the tuk-tuk and rushed through a gateway in the white fortress-like walls.

Inside, Ben stopped in his tracks and let out a whistle.
"Phhheeew! Where are we?"
"This is the Grand Palace," answered Jai.
"Oh, this must be where my dad came to meet with the King," said Ben.
"No," laughed Jai, shaking his head. "King Bhumibol lives somewhere else; this is the home of the past Kings of Thailand."

While searching among the buildings, temples, and shrines, Jai explained further. "You know, Bangkok wasn't always the capital of Thailand. The first was in Sukhothai, in the lower northern region of Thailand, in 1238. But over the years, constant wars with our neighbors forced the capital to keep moving further south: first to Ayutthaya in the upper central region, and then to Thonburi, just across the river from Bangkok. Eventually, in 1782, Bangkok became the capital of Thailand and the new King, Rama I, was the first to live in this palace. But in the 1900's, more modern palaces were constructed elsewhere and the royal family has not lived here since 1925. Our current King Bhumibol, Rama IX, lives in Chitralada Villa. Nowadays, the Grand Palace is still used for royal ceremonies but it's also open as a museum and a tourist attraction."